Travel the World on a Budget

How to Travel Hack the World on a Budget

(How to Cleverly Travel the World on a Shoestring Budget)

Steven Wieland

Published By **Darby Connor**

Steven Wieland

All Rights Reserved

Travel the World on a Budget: How to Travel Hack the World on a Budget (How to Cleverly Travel the World on a Shoestring Budget)

ISBN 978-1-77485-877-6

No part of this guidebook shall be reproduced in any form without permission in writing from the publisher except in the case of brief quotations embodied in critical articles or reviews.

Legal & Disclaimer

The information contained in this ebook is not designed to replace or take the place of any form of medicine or professional medical advice. The information in this ebook has been provided for educational & entertainment purposes only.

The information contained in this book has been compiled from sources deemed reliable, and it is accurate to the best of the Author's knowledge; however, the Author cannot guarantee its accuracy and validity and cannot be held liable for any errors or omissions. Changes are periodically made to this book. You must consult your doctor or get professional medical advice before using any of the suggested remedies, techniques, or information in this book.

Upon using the information contained in this book, you agree to hold harmless the Author from and against any damages, costs, and expenses, including any legal fees potentially resulting from the application of any of the information provided by this guide. This disclaimer applies to any damages or injury caused by the use and application, whether directly or indirectly, of any advice or information presented, whether for breach of contract, tort, negligence, personal injury, criminal intent, or under any other cause of action.

You agree to accept all risks of using the information presented inside this book. You need to consult a professional medical practitioner in order to ensure you are both able and healthy enough to participate in this program.

TABLE OF CONTENTS

Chapter 1: Trip Costs 1

Chapter 2: How You Travel Affects How Much Travelling Will 7

Chapter 3: Solo Travel Vs. Group Travel . 13

Chapter 4: Flights 26

Chapter 5: Accommodation 51

Chapter 6: Food And Activities 66

Chapter 7: Haggling 80

Chapter 8: Work Options Abroad 93

Chapter 9: Truth Of Saving Money 105

Chapter 10: How To Fly Free 144

Chapter 11: The Research 167

Chapter 1: Trip Costs

Before you know how to reduce the cost of travel, you must know all of the costs that come with traveling. In general, when people think of traveling the first thing that comes to mind is an airplane trip to the other side of the world, and I'm here with the truth... plane tickets are expensive. You may be thinking, "Wow so helpful, as if I didn't be aware of that." You probably already knew this, you've been in the world for since at least 18 years and you're probably fully aware that everything is expensive. However, that's not the main point. The main point is that when you don't know how much something will cost you it's impossible to know how much you'll save when you're offered an "good" bargain by an acquaintance or a travel agent or even a website. If you're not able to determine if a deal is a good one whenever you see one, you'll not be in a position to save tons of money when it comes to travel. This is why it's essential to have a complete breakdown of the various costs that come with traveling , before I tell you ways to reduce them by half. I'm not a travel agency. I'm not arranging for you to take the trip of your life It's up to you. The book's goal is to provide is everything you'll need to help you make that happen.

What do we spend money on when traveling? There's a simple answer: the means of getting to where we'd like to go (plane train, bus boat, car or a combination of all or some or any combination of all of them) and a hotel. In any case, these are the two first categories that pop up into our minds.

In the future we'll refer these in the future as flight (this book is focused almost entirely on flights that are cheap over other mode of transport) and accommodations. So, in terms of the accommodation and flights we've worked out:

A) How do I reach there

B) A hotel to stay in when we're there

Now, however, we have to take into consideration everything we'll be spending money on when we arrive in our destination which includes, in general, all the food and drinks we'll consume and all the things we'd like to do during our stay. These categories will be referred to as activities and food.

Although these categories might appear straightforward, they're really quite complex. There are many options to consider before you make your choice so that you be able to better understand what categories you'll invest the majority of your money - but don't worry, I'll assist you to determine how to do which ones by the conclusion in this guide.

In addition, to add a wrench to the whole situation Each of these groups can be viewed in two ways such as solo travel or group travel. That's correct, traveling can cost different amounts of money based on whether you're travelling by you or with an entire group of people.

I'll discuss this further in Chapter 4. However, keep at heart that these tips that are provided throughout the book targeted at solo travel, and thus, are applicable for solo travel in a greater way than group travel. One example my suggestions that I provide later for accommodations is to utilize a website known as Couchsurfing. Although it's not difficult to Couchsurf with two people or more, larger groups of 3 or more could be unable to locate an Couchsurfing host that can accommodate groups of 3 or more. This could seriously impact your budget since Couchsurfing is free, consequently, large numbers of travelers could be required to pay for accommodation to stay (not affordable if you're in a pinch).

This doesn't mean that you can't travel with a group of people on a budget, but it's going to be more difficult than if you were travelling on your own. It's harder however, it's not impossible.

In addition to the costs associated with traveling it is important to consider two additional areas that are extremely important when it comes to calculating the amount of travel that will cost you. These include the ability to bargain and work while traveling. Although neither of these will cost money, they are important to take into consideration when calculating the price of the trip. For instance, if you're traveling to a place where it's not only acceptable and expected to haggle and bargain, you could be able to save some cash and spend less than you planned or get ripped off and pay more than you anticipated, based on your bargaining abilities.

Additionally, if you intend to work while traveling you won't have to put aside the same amount of money before you leave and you'll be more flexible when it comes to your budget. But, if you're likely to earn money while traveling (that's true, it's possible to earn money while you travel).

Travel) and take a variety of decision-making decisions that are budget-conscious to ensure you're aware of the expectations you have for your trip as well as your budget.

Okay, now having examined all the costs related to travel we'll look at the various kinds of trips that you can consider and how your expectations for your trip can significantly impact the amount of money you'll have to spend and, in turn what amount of cash you'll require.

Chapter 2: How You Travel Affects How Much Travelling Will

It will cost you

If you've never been on a trip before, you've probably not considered all the various types of travel options available. For instance, do you think about the mission trip to a third world country identical to the spring break trip to Cancun? No, right? The costs for every type of trip won't be identical either. More than that the price won't be identical It's crucial to consider that the expectations you have for each kind of excursion will also differ greatly. The initial cost associated for each trip will differ due to various reasons (one will likely be scheduled through a third-party entity like a church or any outreach programs and the other one could be scheduled by you or someone else who claimed that they had come across an "great" bargain) Your expectations of each trip as well as what you'd like to do while you're there could differ in significant ways. These variations influence the price of the trip. will cost you.

It's crucial to take into consideration the kind of vacation you'd like take when determining the amount of money you can save, and also where it's feasible in order to reduce costs. i.e. accommodation and flights, food or other activities (if there are any).

There are likely to be hundreds of different kinds of travel that you could take However, I'll focus on the most popular types in this article. However, I won't discuss trips that are usually scheduled through a third party provider (such as the mission trip, tour, trip, cruise or an Groupon offer that covers more than the cost of airfare, etc.) as you won't normally save money on accommodations and travel on these kinds of travels and, really they aren't the types of trips that college students purchasing this book will most likely be taking anyways (although in the event that you're broke and end up taking any of those trips, for any reason, the suggestions I provide for eating out and other activities could be helpful to you).

Now that we've shown that travel is something more than just an holiday, let's discuss the various types of trips that you can make as a college student. While it's possible to enjoy a low-cost trip (1-2 weeks) but this isn't the most suitable option for college students.

are looking to experience long-term travel. If you would like to travel for more than 10 or a week It is also possible to look into volunteering in another country or immersive cultural experiences (through homestays or exchange programs, or Couchsurfing) as well as studying abroad.

I'm not going into too many details in this book on students' options to study abroad because every school and student is unique and the office for study abroad at your school is far more knowledgeable than I have ever. Therefore, I suggest to visit your school's study abroad center and, as a rule of thumb, you should consider going abroad to "unpopular" destinations like Eastern Europe, lesser known countries that are located in Asia, Central America and even Africa. The less popular a nation is, the more affordable it's likely to be.

Also, I'm going give this advice because I'd feel like an insufferable if I didn't however, I'd like you to know that you're not under any obligation to follow my advice, and I'm not responsible for any harm you suffer in the wake of following my advice. Now having removed that disclaimer from the way, here's a point you should be aware of when selecting an international study program. I suggest studying abroad during the second year of your college. Here's the reason Federal student aid will generally not apply to studies abroad during the semester unless the student is enrolled in one of the majors that requires the student to devote time studying abroad before graduating.

This is right, you could use federal student aid to help you achieve your travel goals when it turns out that you feel that the program you're currently enrolled in "just isn't the right one to you" and you'd prefer to look into a different field to determine if that's the right fit for you. *Cough cough * The principal word here is to attempt. Within your first two years of university, you are able to transfer majors without much impact on the date you graduate. Once you've "tried" the major you're interested in perhaps you'll decide that, "you know what, it's not for me at all" and you'll be able to change back to your first major. So that's what I'll say about studying abroad in the rest of the book. There is no obligation to follow any of the suggestions offered in this book. I am in no way financially or legally responsible for any adverse results you could face as consequence of following my suggestions. Be intelligent Keep your mouth shut and don't tell anyone in the administration of your school the reason behind your decision to change majors.

Okay, to return to the right course, traveling is more than just a vacation; it could be a complete experience, a chance to do something, volunteer and meet new people, or start studying the language of your choice. It could be a long-term experience. It is also possible to be a short-term. It's a good reason to enjoy a international beer in a different city. Travel is all about how you define it. Whatever, this book will assist you in making it happen on low cost.

Chapter 3: Solo Travel Vs. Group Travel

Another factor that could influence the price of your travel is whether you decide to travel on your own or with your friends (or some other type of group individuals). While I'm an avid advocate of traveling alone however, it doesn't mean that it's always the most economical option. However, there are times when travelling with a group could cost less; two phrases: group discounts. That's why it's vital to consider this when deciding the price of your travel.

This is the reason I'll go through the advantages and disadvantages (with regards to cost only) of traveling on your own or having an entire group.

Solo Travel

Pros:

1.) There is no need to think about finding the right to ___ (food seating, seats, availability etc.) just for one, making getting things done in the last minute simpler. It can also be economical as, for instance you'll be able get the last seat on the cheapest bus, rather than needing to travel on the bus with a higher price that offers more seats. Solo travel is more affordable to make last-minute decisions.

2.) Many of the tools I'll be discussing during Chapter 6 will be more straightforward to access when you're traveling on your own. As I've mentioned before that it's easier to locate an Couchsurfing host when you're just one person. Additionally, it's simpler to find a hostel that only requires one volunteer as opposed to a hostel which requires 3 or more volunteers.

3.) It's much easier to locate an airline ticket that is discounted as opposed to numerous discounted flights as airlines are able to reduce one class of fare until there are no more tickets for the class (which implies that you'll likely be able to find the last tickets available). Although that may not be a good idea for all people however, this isn't a complete review of airfare prices and pricing, so you should inquire about the different classes of airfare and how airlines price their tickets, keep reading.

Based on these classes, you should definitely do further research on Google. It's too complicated to cover in this post and it's not really worth the effort. What you must know about traveling for a low price is that you shouldn't just be happy because you bought a flight ticket at $60.

It doesn't mean you'll manage to purchase 6 tickets at the same price of just $60.

4.) When traveling by yourself, it will not necessarily result in food being more affordable, it can allow you to buy food at a lower cost because you only need to take into consideration one person's tastes desires, preferences, and appetite. You can enjoy the cheap street food that you can find, or you can purchase food items and cook at home if the location you're located has a kitchen accessible to you. You could decide to not even eat in case you don't consider yourself starving at the time. It's all up to you , and you are in complete control of the amount you spend, what you eat and the frequency you consume food.

5) This is the same for actions. You are in total control. You are only doing the things you'd like to take part in and don't need to take part in activities simply because that's what everybody else would like to do.

6.) It's also simpler to find a job for only one person rather than for multiple people living in the same area. It's also highly likely that all of your group will be offered the job you applied for, which means that the original plans for travel need to be reviewed and possibly even negatively affected (depending the tight knit nature of your group is as well as the manner in which the person you're with is considerate of the rest of the group).

Cons:

1.) If this is your first time particularly if you're a woman, it might be a good idea to pay more to ensure your security. It's possible due to personal reasons to spend more on accommodation to feel more secure. It's not a bad thing. It's not ideal that you travel to a new place that you feel so uneasy and worried about your security or the security of your belongings that you are unable to enjoy your trip. The level of safety that each person has is different , and so it is important to take this into account when making plans for your travel plans. This could be an area that you aren't willing to reduce costs to save money.

Well-being and mental health.

2) You don't get group discounts... ever. It's all on your own and even if you do find some friends to share a space with (Which you will definitely do regardless of whether you're

usually an extrovert. If you're travelling on your own for long enough, you'll be craving human contact to the point that it'll make you to form friendships.) It's likely that group discounts won't prove so lucrative for last-minute travel plans and there may not be discounts for groups available.

3.) If you're a sucker for haggling but do not have someone with you to help and ensure you're getting the best price You could be viewed as an swindler and getting overcharged for something you'd like or need to purchase. This is only the case when you're in a place in which it's normal and accepted to haggle.

Group Travel

Pros:

1.) All group discounts. You'll be able to easily contact the person in charge of an thing you and your buddies are looking to participate in or the day trip you'd like to take and negotiate to get a better rate if there's an entire group (or If you're lucky there are discounts for groups that may already be available). Additionally, staying at an Airbnb could be more affordable because the expense will be divided among the group of. If you are staying in hostels, you may be able to afford the privacy of your room(s) as, again the cost is split across the group of.

2.) In an entire group, you could not be as concerned about safety, and thus you won't have to pay more costs for lodging within those "best" or "safest" areas. If you are in a group, then you'll be able to guarantee your safety in a majority of areas which means you can concentrate all your efforts on finding the most affordable bargain.

3.) If one of you hates haggling, there is a person in your group who is a pro at haggling. The person who is great at haggling can be the one to take over and haggle for all of you at any time

Anyone who wants to buy something. So everyone in the group enjoys a bargain on what they require or want to purchase. It's true that this is only valid in countries where it's a common custom to bargain.

Cons:

1.) It isn't enough to buy the lowest price ticket or book the room with the lowest price. It is essential to ensure that there are plenty of beds or tickets to accommodate all. It could cost you more over the long haul because great airfare rates particularly are usually only applicable to a few tickets.

2.) As I've already mentioned it's difficult to locate Couchsurfing hosts who have enough space to accommodate a whole crowd of individuals. This can have a significant impact on your budget because Couchsurfing is free. Additionally, Workaway is more convenient by having just one person because farms and hostels do not often require assistance by more than three individuals at once (however it is possible to be lucky and it's a good idea to keep an eye on).

3.) Although you may enjoy having street food at home, perhaps some of your acquaintances are vegan while another is gluten-free and the other isn't a fan of vegetables. Instead of choosing the one that is the cheapest and easiest it is essential to locate an eatery that can accommodate all tastes and needs. And who can claim that everyone will feel hungry during different time of the day? If someone is so hungry they're hungry, it's likely they'll make you consume food wherever it is convenient regardless of price. In this case it's possible that you don't even enjoy the food you eat and, in that case, you've just spent your money on something that did not even like.

4.) This is also true for activities. If you're in a group of people, you may find yourself doing things (and spending money for it) which you're not keen on or you could have, if given the option that you wouldn't do when you were on your own. To me, this is a waste of time and money. I have met a woman recently who was in Belize who was taking a cave tour at San Ignacio who was a poor swimmer, was claustrophobic and did not like dark. The cave tour was not her favorite however, she had been coerced into it by the group she was traveling with. This excursion cost $75.

While her friends could have enjoyed themselves but it was a total wasted time for her. The money she spent but she wasn't enjoying herself, and spent the day in Belize.

5) It's harder to find work in a large group of individuals. If this is how you planned to go on vacation, you may need to alter your plans if the group is unable to find work.

The advantages and disadvantages of travelling on your own or with a group of friends is only with regard to finances and planning your travel plans. It doesn't consider the personality type of your guests or the amount of enjoyment you'll experience if you travel with your most cherished acquaintances or any other aspect of any type of trip that's difficult to assign a value on. But, these factors are important to take into consideration.

We've now covered everything we need to take into consideration before deciding the amount the trip will cost and what choices are most suitable in terms of choosing flights and accommodations and planning for meals and other activities.

The next chapter may be the one you've been waiting for to know the best resources and tricks you can employ to save money on travel and score great deals. It's crucial to read the initial chapters as they will serve as the foundation for the details I'll be giving you regarding cheap travel. If you don't understand the various aspects of travel and how different your travel experiences can be based on your personal preferences and what you're looking for, you could utilize every advice and guide I provide and still feel disappointed by your travels because your expectations were not in alignment with the decisions you made, and also the areas you could have cut costs. I once flew for 10 hour to Los Angeles to Reykjavik on an airline that was low-cost and had no facilities (no television or entertainment system or food service and no blankets or pillows... Nothing extra) simply because it was just $99. However, I knew the kind of thing I was in for so I didn't feel dissatisfied or angry. I planned my trip according to my needs and ensured that I was exhausted at the time I got on the plane that I'd be asleep for the whole flight. Keep in mind that when you're considering budget travel, it's crucial to ensure that your expectations align with your choices. The cost of budget travel is extremely entertaining and a memorable adventure,

But not if you are spending your entire time thinking you were at an elite hotel and sipping champagne.

This is the reason for the final three chapters to ensure that you're in the journey with eyes and make educated decisions in light of your personality and what you can and can't manage. Remember that your experience on the road is based on how well you've defined your expectations and how transparent your self-respect. If you don't have any expectations and the less you have to worry about, the better your trip will be.

Chapter 4: Flights

The first thing to think about when planning an excursion is to figure out how you'll arrive at where you'd like to be. Because this book is focused upon international travel, the entire section is devoted to finding low-cost flights and the strategies and tips you can employ to ensure that you get the best deal.1

1.) Take the time to do Your Research If you have a location you're thinking of (or maybe a few that are appealing to you) check out the web right now and research flights prices.2 Take a look at the amount the flight to your destination is for 4 months out and 2 months out. 1 month out, and two weeks out. See the prices change based on what you search for. If you're using an online search engine, such as Google flights it will show you the cost all month in the vicinity of the date you're searching for. It will provide you with an idea of what an "good" price would be for the flight you're looking for and will help you be able to recognize an GREAT deal when you find one. Be aware that when you're not able to afford lots of money, you must compensate by having an abundance of knowledge (and this applies to every aspect of your life).

2.) Create an Alert for Flights 2) Use airfare watchdog, to have flight alerts directly to your email address on the flight that you are interested. Airfare Watchdog doesn't only inform you that the price is dropping and then when it goes up also. This is a great option if you're just beginning since you'll begin to be aware of how fast prices for flights can alter. This happens due to the fact that it creates a sense of urgency within the consumer. Uninformed customers, who do not know the difference between a great bargain and a normal (or somewhat expensive) price, are likely to buy as quickly as they can in fear that the cost increases. Pay attention to your airfare watchdog alerts , and you'll notice that there's a bonus tip: Once you've gotten there, you can take advantage of ridesharing services to cut down on expenses. Look at websites like: erideshare.com, compartir.org and hitchhikers.org 2 Make sure when looking for flights or hotels that you always use the private tab (or erase and deactivate cookies). The airlines and other companies can utilize your search history to disadvantage you and raise the price of a hotel or flight that they believe you are keen on... And they can tell because you've already searched for it at least a couple of times.

3 When looking for flights that go to a specific destination, make sure you're using an entire location (meaning that all airports in the vicinity are included) instead of one particular airport, as this can increase the likelihood of finding a lower-cost ticket.

Prices for airfares aren't always linear. they don't continue to rise when they begin to rise and they don't continue to fall after they've begun to fall. They're very sporadic, which is why the initial step is crucial to ensure that when you find an amazing deal, you are able to grab it without doubt or buyer's remorse.4

3.) Make sure you check multiple Travel Search Engines though airfare watchdog gives you a fantastic price on an airfare, you must take a look for other engines in order to determine which ones have a more attractive price. The search engines I use the most often are Google Flights (this is my preferred search engine, and I'll tell you why in a moment), Momondo, Kayak, Skyscanner, Vayama, Hipmunk and Travelocity. Doing a quick lookup on these sites could bring you an extra $10-$30 off a already amazing bargain.

4.) Use Google Flights: Google flights is an amazing search engine that is based on a single feature You can view the prices of airfare from a perspective of a map and determine the cost to travel to the places near where you are for the dates you searched. To break it into pieces to make it easier to comprehend I'll give some examples. In order to simplify I'm going to be the one-way route.

4. You can also create email alerts for "mistake prices" as well as flight deals, to ensure that you're always on top of the latest airfares, no matter the destination (although you're able to set an airport for departure). Visit: secretflying.com, theflightdeal.com and nextvacay.com

Okay, in this image you can see that) It's a personal browser to look up my flights (the blue search bar with the black color is the main offer) and the second) I'm trying to find an all-in one plane between Los Angles to Rome. After I enter your date Google gives me an overview of calendars that allows me to look at the month in which I am and the next month. This is where I can see that when I fly on the 18th of September it's most affordable. cheapest.5 Google made finding the lowest price for me by making it easier for me by turning the text green to indicate the lowest price. Since 5 is my apology for the symbols of the pound. The place I'm from is Antigua, Guatemala and to ensure that I could view the site in English I checked the UK

Google version: Google: Google.co.uk, since Google.com only brings up Google.co.uk, which is the Google search engine of the country you're located in. There's probably an option to access the American version however, I'm not tech-savvy. After all the time I've spent traveling I'm a pro with conversion rates , so this is simply a method that is very effective for me. For your convenience, I've provided the conversion rate to American currency, as on August 4, 2017. (the day I did this search).

This is all about low-cost airfare. I'm planning to pick this date for my departure point and check to see if I can find an alternative that is cheaper.

From this image you can clearly see, if I depart on the 18th of May, Norwegian airline is offering an offer of PS214 (which will cost $279) The next best flight is Aeroflot at PS389 ($507) This is more expensive then PS100 ($130). What you will also notice in this image is that in the upper right corner an icon for a map which is the instrument which will assist you in saving a lot of dollars on airfare6.

6 Although this tool has allowed me to save money every time I've paid for an airline ticket (i.e. I didn't have rewards points/miles) The real savings occur when you book a bit further.

Since Rome is my ultimate destination, I'll need to focus on Europe and check out the other prices available. However, if you look carefully you can also find airfare rates for any other destination around the world at the date of this post. Without needing to zoom in I am able to see that a flight for Mexico City only costs PS86 ($112) If I wanted to, I could visit Panama City for only PS149

($194) and each of London and Stockholm (both are PS185 ($241). If you're flexible about the places you'd like to go however you're not flexible about the time you're able to travel the map tool is an incredible tool. However, let's return to the illustration. Let's focus on Europe.

Also I can observe the fact that taking a flight to London seems to be the most affordable method of traveling into Europe starting from Los Angeles, along with Dublin, Brussels, and Berlin. Even though Paris, Frankfurt, Amsterdam and Madrid aren't that far more costly. However, after many years of traveling to Europe and booking tickets to planes in and throughout Europe I'm aware that I should be focusing on London since it's going to be the most likely place that will offer low-cost flights to Rome. Don't be discouraged as this is a normal thing that happens over the course of years of looking for flights. If you're just beginning, you'll be able to open the new tab and go through each of these sites to determine which one has the most affordable airfare to Rome at the time you'd like to fly into and, to be honest even though I'd definitely investigate London first, as I'm pretty sure that London will be my top choice, I'd be foolish to not check all the other cities for the possibility that they offer a fantastic deal on the table as well. When it comes to airfare, you don't know, and it takes just a little effort to go an extra mile to check that it's a mistake to not do it.

When I look up London (since there is already a separate window open, I simply start a new tab in my private browser) I can see that I can travel to Rome at a cost of PS22 ($28) every day beginning on the 18th until the 21st of September. This means that I can decide to fly directly to London to Rome at a cost of PS7 ($9) less than flying directly to Rome or visit two cities during my travels by staying for several days in London prior to going to Rome and still pay the price of PS7 ($9) less. Whichever way you choose, you'll save money.7

7 I realize that $9 isn't an enormous amount of money even by an imagination. However, I wanted to provide you with an idea of a last minute flight idea. I simply picked an unrelated destination to search for a flight, and I wanted to show you that it is always an option to make savings. I've utilized this exact method before and saved hundreds of dollars

in airfare. My friend recently contacted me for assistance because she was planning to bring his boyfriend on a trip to Barcelona to celebrate his birthday, however, she could not find anything within her budget. The cheapest roundtrip tickets she could find were priced at about 800 dollars. Since she had flexibility about her travel dates (as as long as it was within 1-3 weeks of the birthday of her boyfriend) I was able to utilize the same method I'm going to outline for you within this section to save her $300 for each ticket by taking she through Paris. My friend not only save more than $600 on her flights by herself, she also had the opportunity to spend 3 days Paris together with her partner and eight additional nights in Barcelona.

However, as I stated it's a mistake to not check out the other cities So I did, and like I was expecting the cities were all expensive to travel to Rome. The costs varied widely from

PS46 ($59) to PS99 ($129). Thus traveling into London at first will be the most affordable option.8

This is why I am a huge fan of my Google Flights search engine tool to the fullest. The flexibility it gives in the search for flights allows you to locate the most affordable alternative and even travel to one or two additional cities because of it.

5.) Make sure to check to see if you can use the Roundtrip Option: Make sure you always check the roundtrip option, because you'll be amazed by how much you could save by flying roundtrip! 9 Utilizing the same scenario like before, let's look at the cost of an roundtrip flight between Los Angeles to London. It's based on decades of experience and the intuition that this roundtrip is substantially cheaper than a direct roundtrip to Rome on identical dates. But it is true that even after doing this for a long time (and since I've been doing it for many years) I always check to make sure. As I've previously discussed with you, prices for airfare can fluctuate at any time either way and you don't are aware of when the perfect offer will be available and you should always be on the lookout.

When I search for a round-trip flights to LA to London and back, I see: 8 Most of the time, it's cheaper to fly first into London in anywhere in the U.S. city, and later travel from London (for European destinations), however there are many variations and I've flown into numerous European cities before settling for the most affordable airfare and don't follow this blindly. It's something more like a fashion, not true.

Nine Pro Tips: Sometimes, the roundtrip route is more affordable than the one-way alternative. Always verify.

On the 18th of May, prices are advertised as PS323 ($421). This is less expensive than purchasing two tickets one-way, as the flight that was one-way between LA to London cost PS214 ($279) as well as 279 2.

558. With this price it would save us $137 by booking the roundtrip (although it only applies if you actually depart from London and return towards LA). Be aware that the price of your return tickets needs to be at par with the price so if you choose the return date, it doesn't include PS323 You'll pay the more expensive price. We'll check to ensure that the round trip won't cost more.

Awesome! This means that we could return to any of the dates in green and pay the same price as advertised when we decided to leave at the end of 18th. In this scenario, I picked the 29th as it's the one that appeals for me (I prefer longer journeys in comparison to short ones). After I've selected the date of my return, this is what comes up:

This proves that in fact, I'll pay PS323 ($421) to purchase an all-round ticket that connects LA to London.

Additionally I mentioned earlier that because of my experience with travel and the various hub cities, I came to an assumption that a trip roundtrip between LA and London on those dates would cost less than a roundtrip flight between LA or Rome. However, as I've mentioned before, it's nothing more work to do a quick search and it would be foolish not to. Let's take a look at the price for round trips from LA and Rome for the same dates.

As you will see, the price for this particular flight is much more expensive. But, it's worth checking since there is no way to know for sure. It could be half the price in LA and London depending on the availability of a sale for an unknown airline such as Emirates as well as Aer Lingus. It's impossible to know for sure, which is why this is why you do your research.

Back to the price that flies between LA and London It's an excellent deal. This isn't the best deal I've seen, but certainly the most affordable particularly since it's the flight to take place in just six weeks from when I first looked it up. You'll be flying to Europe and returning for just $421. I've done it less than $325. I know others who have

The cost was about 200 dollars (on the wrong price) So you're aware that $421 is a great price in terms of cheap airfare is concerned (especially when there's no promotion or sale taking place).

6.) If the price is right... Book It's so crucial. If the price is reasonable and it's not expensive and within the budget of yours, as well as suitable for the dates you'd like (if there's no flexibility in your schedule) If so, then you should make the booking. Don't delay; don't give yourself just a "couple number of weeks" to consider it. I cannot stress this enough that airfare prices fluctuate ALL The Time. Airlines can alter their rates at any time in response to a myriad of different factors. If you discover a fantastic bargain and wait for a while, the flight will be more expensive once you attempt to purchase it. That's why it's important to follow the steps that I've described in the previous paragraphs. When you are booking your flight, you must be certain that you've got the best price for the destination and time you choose to travel. I don't want you be remorseful about buying. Instead I want you to boast to your friends about how low your airfare was for your trip.

These are the steps I take when booking flights generally, I would like to give you a few suggestions to help you get the lowest price possible on your flights and even fly for no cost.

If you adhere to the steps that I've mentioned in the previous paragraphs and consider these guidelines in consideration while planning your next trip, you'll never have to pay for flights ever for airfare ever again.

TIP #1: Be flexible in your travel plans, or when you travel. If you are able to be flexible on at most one of these things the two, you'll always be able to get a great deal on airfare. Bonus tip If you're flexible in both WHEN and WHERE you will get a bargain on flights. For instance, I learned that WOW air offered a promo for one-way flights for $99 that run from Los Angeles to Reykjavik, Iceland.

Do I have plans to travel to Iceland prior to learning about the promo? No. It was a surprise to hear about it. Absolutely! Absolutely! I'll travel anyplace if the price is just $99. (I am referring to the fact that it may be more expensive to travel between LA in the direction of Las Vegas, and that flight isn't much more than one hour.) But here's the thing, the promotion was not available for each day of the week. There were specific dates (throughout the next few months) where the promotion price was applied. This is the thing I am talking about of being flexible with the location you travel to and when.

you go. This isn't the best option for everyone, which is why I began this article by saying you should be flexible in at the very least one. Being flexible is essential in securing the best deals on flights.

Tip #2: Make sure to reserve at a minimum of 2 weeks (seriously that's the absolute minimum required to secure a fair price, but ONLY if your flexible on the time or location) at least a month in advance.

When you are booking your airfare, it is best to avoid extremes Don't make a booking too far in advance, and don't do it too late. You should create your watchdog alerts for your airfare at least six months prior to departure (If you're able, though I've booked extremely cheap flights in the past without taking the time to create a watchdog alert.) It is recommended to book your flight no earlier than three to four months ahead and no later than 2 weeks ahead. Last minute deals DO

It's possible, but the chance that you'll see one exactly where you'd like to go is low.

Third tip: It one might be obvious But I'm going add it When you can, try not to fly during the weekend. Weekend flights, i.e. Friday nights and Sundays are typically more expensive. If you are able take flights on Thursday and return in the week, or Saturday, even. Although technically, Saturday is regarded as a weekend however when it comes to flights Saturdays can be either as it may be costly or be the most affordable option, it's just a matter of.

Tips #4 is related to what I taught you about how to utilize Google flights with their map tool. Pretty often you shouldn't take direct flights. Sometimes, the most economical alternative is to fly across other major cities. It's easy to do this by using your Google flight search tool. Sometimes , however, you'll see prices that are offered to you but aren't direct flights. It could be that the airline doesn't provide an direct flight between the two destinations and/or the engine that you used attempted to find an affordable price using routing through a different city.

Tip #5: Only bring carry-on luggage. If you just pack one carry-on bag, you don't need to pay extra charges for baggage that you check in. Be sure to check for the policy of the company you have booked with to find out whether you are allowed to check a bag free of charge and if not (this is typically based on the way you travel).

how far you're flying) and adjust the price accordingly. The most affordable rates are found with the so-called low-cost airlines (i.e. Ryanair, Wowair, Easyjet, etc.) And what is low-cost for these airlines in that they do not provide a large number of extras and you'll have pay for an additional checked bag and entertainment, food as well as other things. If you're not able to get an unchecked bag at no cost then take a 5-minute Youtube video tutorial on how to prepare your luggage as a flight attendant, and, I'm sure, you'll have everything you require to make your travels. Really, with this advice there's really no excuse. I'm currently traveling for the next six years, and all I've got in my bag is a big backpack and a duffel bag Not just that I'm carrying everything I require for working abroad, but I also have more than 10 days of clothing as well as a full year's supply of contacts and medicine along with some cosmetics and toiletries. It's possible I am confident in your abilities.

Tip #6: I cannot overstate this enough (seriously I'm sure I've already mentioned this, but it's worth it add it again if it prompts you to take action) When you're looking for flights or hotels/hostels, you should make sure you use a separate window. If you don't own the luxury of a Mac then you should erase your cookies and then disable them. The airlines don't need to be aware of how interested you are about flying to this or that location, as should they find out it, they'll raise the cost: if the demand for something rises and the cost goes up, so does the demand.

Tip #7: Fly in the off-season. Not only will you receive the lowest price on flights, but you'll also enjoy discounts on accommodations where you can stay as well as local attractions and excursions. And as an added benefit you'll see less people - which means more photos and fewer crowds. Remember that the cost is a function of the amount of demand. If you visit a place in a period when many tourists are visiting, prices will fall due to the lower demand.

In particular, if you're located in a place in which it's normal to haggle and bargain, you'll have more leverage as the seller won't have the capacity to make a lot of sales in one day and will be willing to offer you the best price in order to win an order.

Tip #8: Watch for sales. Airlines often offer promo rates to boost the sales of flights that don't generate an abundance of income. Low-cost carriers are particularly popular for their dirt cheap sales rates. For example, travel blogger Adventurous Kate

I once found a deal that took you on a flight from Milan from Milan to Budapest and from Budapest to Milan Budapest to Paris for just 1 cent on Wizzair which is exactly one cent. After taxes, the price was 45 euros, but it's still an amazing deal for two flights, and the entire 45 euros was tax (which are required for most flights anyways). The most affordable carriers include Ryanair, Easyjet, Wizzair, Wowair, Southwest, and Jetblue (although there are numerous more). Additionally, Virgin Australia offers happy hourly rates for an hour every day. It is a good idea to become familiar with low-cost airlines that operate out of the closest airport to you and keep on top of their sales and promotions.

Tip #9: Consider booking using the local currency. It means, for instance, that the company you have found the price originates located in Turkey or Ireland or the UAE for instance go to the Turkish or Irish as well as it's Emirati site (rather instead of the American version that is written in English and shows price that are in USD) to determine whether, based on the current day's conversion rate, your price is less expensive in the currency of the origin. This could save you a few dollars , on top of all of the other tricks I've given you, and believe me when I say $5 here and $3 here is a lot of money.

Here and there, $15 really can add up to make a significant saving.

Tip #10 The biggest tip, the most crucial and complicated advice of them all. Actually, this technique could fill up the entire book by itself that's why I'm launching another ebook that does this. Are you are ready? Here's the information: Take advantage of airline reward programs. While this might seem ridiculously easy to accomplish It's not just a simple signing up for the airline rewards program. It's about understanding the specifics of each reward program and the way co-branded credit cards could allow you to travel around across the globe for no cost. It's been a long time since I've traveled for the last five years and paid just the taxes that I pay for the flights. This is right, I took business class flights to Switzerland from LA just two summers ago. I only paid taxes of $300... to take a business class for an international flight. In spring, I took a roundtrip flight to Portugal for just 50 dollars in tax. I've travelled across all across the continent of

United States on Southwest for just $7 in taxes per flight. Los Angeles to Vegas $7, Los Angeles to New Orleans $7. You'll get the idea. Naturally, this can be EXTREMELY profitable. But, it's also very complex. Be sure to keep an eye on

to finish my ebook on how to make the most of your daily spending to get free flights to anywhere in the globe!

Chapter 5: Accommodation

There are a lot of alternatives to save money for accommodation during travel I'm going break the chapter in two major sections: accommodation for free and low-cost accommodation. There are many distinctions, not just in the sections but equally between the options available within each section. I make every effort to explain every option as thorough as I can, but I'm clearly more inclined to go with the options I'm more comfortable with. I'm going to be completely transparent about this prior to diving into this chapter to ensure you know what I'm talking about when I go over the ways you can reside in a different country without cost or low cost.

Before I start, I need to remind you one to remember that should you travel during the off season , everything will be less expensive and not just airfares as well as the accommodation. Be aware of this as you consider all the options I'm going to offer you.

Because this book is detailing traveling as a student who is broke without a dime I'm going start with a list of no-cost lodging choices. You bought this book in order to could travel around the world for little or no cash.

Free Accommodation

I'm planning to further separate this section into no-strings-attached free lodging to simplify things and help you to browse through the options I'm going to offer to help you find the one that works best for you.

House Sitting

Another option for staying no cost in different countries would be to let your house sit. There are many websites that connect prospective house sitters to people who need someone to watch at their home and perhaps keep a few plants watered when they're away. Remember that the majority of these websites require a fee to "join" and then become a certified house sitter. But, this isn't the case in all cases.

you'll also benefit since it guarantees that the individuals you'll be assisting will also be confirmed.

The verification process provides an additional security measure to ensure that nobody is, regardless of the housesitter or the owner of the property or the house, is an axe-murderer. But seriously, the verification is just to make sure that the person who is enrolled is who they claim to be. are. In most cases, you'll pay with the credit or debit card. The name you provide to the organization must be the same as the card and the other details you provide.

Websites to join if you're interested in house sitting are: Housesittersamerica.com

Mindmyhouse.com

Trustedhousesitters.com

Nomador.com

Housecarers.com

It is also possible to search for specific websites for house sitters in your country. For instance, if would like the house sitter job in Australia then visit:

Housesitworld.com.au

Happyhousesitters.com.au

Aussiehousesitters.com.au

When you pay the one-time cost to join any of these associations that allow house sitting for anyone who is a part of that community (which implies that you'd surely be interested in joining the website that has the greatest reach) at no cost. Even though it is only a once-off cost for this, I've included it in the no-cost accommodation since after paying this fee, it's cost-free and you'll get an entire home to yourself in the country you choose. Remember this as I talk about the no-strings-attached choices as everyone has various levels of security. For instance, someone like me who is among the most private people you'll meet, might not think it worthwhile to pay a single fee to rent a whole house for me (for no cost) during my travels but someone else could think it's a bargain particularly since the costs aren't that expensive and it's a once-only thing.

No-Strings-Attached

These are the no-hassle options I would prefer. You don't need to work to find a place to stay or pay any fees (not even a single fee). You sign up, you locate an individual to live with, and then you leave. Websites that let you stay at no cost with locals in many countries include: Couchsurfing.org

Globalfreeloaders.com

Hospitalityclub.org

Stay4free.com

I'm going be transparent about this. The only of these alternatives I have any personal knowledge of is Couchsurfing. However, I am a firm supporter of Couchsurfing. I've had amazing experiences Couchsurfing and, honestly I would prefer it if you offered me the choice between staying in an Airbnb or Couchsurfing then I'll pick Couchsurfing every time (even even if you said that Airbnb would be completely free). This is my absolute favorite method of travel.

TRAVEL.

Let me get honest with you. If you Couchsurf (or any option) you're staying at an entirely stranger's home in a foreign land. It is imperative to erase everything your mother ever taught you about strangers and remove the term "stranger danger" from your mental memory bank. Let me speak from personal experience as a woman - not only a single person however, as an individual woman who Couchsurfed on a solo trip and isn't any more than a little risky If you adhere to my suggestions. Again I Couchsurfed in a solo travel as a woman, and the most of the Couchsurfing hosts were males. The Couchsurfing experience was always amazing that the majority of these guys are my best friends until this day, and I am in constant contact with them. (And it could be considered a bit tinny however it's crucial to understand that - in order to fully appreciate the awesomeness of Couchsurfing is.) I've did not sleep with anyone members of the Couchsurfing hosts. It was a personal choice. I'm sure a lot of them would be all too willing to accommodate me if I'd decided to. But I didn't. They did their best to make my time memorable and special. If you're a woman, do not think that you are required to

Sleep with your hosts if you do not want to do so simply because they're staying at their house at no cost. (That's not the purpose of Couchsurfing can be.) I can't emphasize this enough. Couchsurfing is an amazing option for broke College students.

This is my suggestion if you're contemplating Couchsurfing as well as any websites which are basically similar to Couchsurfing:

1.) Don't join a group that doesn't have positive reviews by other Couchsurfers (this is particularly crucial for women traveling on your own). I've have never Couchsurfed with a guy who didn't have five positive, relevant reviews from women who have also viewed his profile.

The most important factor to remember when Couchsurfing is safety. Anything is possible to increase your safety must. When I first started , I even reached out to reviewers to find out more about their experience in the company of their host.

If you tell them that you're just beginning to learn about Couchsurfing and you're just looking for to know what is expected, they'll be very understanding and will be able to answer your questions. Don't be afraid of ask them the questions you're thinking about. When I first started , I asked women if they had slept with the man who hosted them and if they were drinking when they did. I also inquired if. If they had the chance, they'd return to the host. Ask all the questions you can make sure you feel confident with your decision.10

2.) Talk to the person prior to going to their house more than simply the initial, "Can I stay at your house" and, in turn, "Yes you can." You must talk to this person, and be open and transparent about your expectations and the things is acceptable to you. If you'd like someone to take you around, or people to hang out with Let them know. If you're just looking for a place to stay, but don't wish to spend a lot of time with someone tell them. It's more enjoyable if you are open about what you expect in the beginning and, the moment you arrive there's nothing to worry about. are also able to get verified by Couchsurfing for just $60 (and hosts can be verified too). However, it's true that verification has was never a major factor for me. I've been with people who were not verified and did not get verified because I was trying to save cash.

There was a miscommunication, and nobody was expecting something else.

When I first Couchsurfed I was just 19 years old. I informed the person who allowed me to remain in his home that I'd never done it before, and that I was a bit nervous and unsure of my choice. Instead of being annoyed or refusing my request the man was incredibly

awesome. He provided me with his address for his personal use months in advance of the date to hand over to my parents since they were also concerned. He also let me provide my parents with the email addresses (in the case that there was emergencies) and we talked lot in the months prior to when I arrived to ensure it was possible for me to come meet him. When I finally arrived at his home in London it was more than if I had been visiting an old friend.

I'm saying this because I want to stress that you must only choose what is comfortable for you. I was aware that I would like to Couchsurf since it was going be a great way to save money, however, I was aware of the reality that I'd not traveled before and did not want anything to happen to me because of my foolishness. If this is your first experience take your time and be extremely be cautious. This is the most beneficial thing that you could make for your self. In the past I've had some extraordinary experiences Couchsurfing which I would not be able to have otherwise. I was chauffeured through Florence in the back of an Vespa and stayed with an Couchsurfing hosts who resided in the top floor of the pizzeria that he worked in Pizza every night I'm sure! I went to an establishment in Austria which was run by the Couchsurfing host's pal and was given unlimited drinks throughout the night and had the opportunity to make my own cocktails. I was fortunate that my Couchsurfing hosts in Rome prepared me pasta for the first night I was in Italy with his grandmother's home-cooked olive oil (and it was the most delicious pasta I've ever had and since). Also, I've not been forced to lie down on couches.

The majority of the time, the time, your Couchsurfing host has a spare room that you can sleep in, with an extra bed as well as a lockable door. So I DEFINITELY recommend Couchsurfing. It's free. It's fun. It's great if you're broke.

Cheap Hotel Accommodation

Okay, now that you're aware of the options for free I'm going to offer those who want to know the "cheap" alternatives.

Naturally, they will cost you money , and while I was in college, it was free cheaper than a lot, but I'm gonna include these anyway so that you're able to make your own decision.

The alternatives you should be considering when you are looking for a cheap hotel are: Airbnb.com

Wimdu.com

Homestay.com

9flats.com

Hostelworld.com

Hostels.com

Most people are familiar with Airbnb by now and I won't get into too much detail regarding that. Wimdu and 9flats are the same as Airbnb (it's the distinction from Google Bing and Google). Bing).

Homestay is basically Couchsurfing which you pay for. Or If you're looking to compare it with Airbnb It's similar to an Airbnb that the person who owns the house that you are staying at actually talks to you and invites you to their home. They spend the time you spend with them. In either case, you'll have be paying for the service. The other two choices are hostels. Similar to Couchsurfing I'm going to talk about hostels very fast because I'm sure they've got poor reputation, and I'd like to give you the chance to decide from personal experiences.

Similar to Couchsurfing I've been to several hostels. They weren't all great, but you are paying for what you receive. What I mean is that I've stayed in the hostels for parties that had bars attached to them which I couldn't sleep, and also in which I'm sure some of the guests were in the hostel (definitely not individuals, and specifically males that I would have been able to identify with in other ways) as well as in hostels that were superior to others I've stayed in. The price of a hostel does not only depend on the cleanliness or how secure you feel it's the location you're in. For instance I've stayed in affordable hostels across Southeast Asia that were really lovely and even had breakfast. I've also stayed at more expensive hostels in Europe that were more filthy and more of a "party"

crowd. The location you travel to can affect the experience you have at your hostel.

However, regardless of the destination, be sure to review the hostel to see what others have to say about the place and ensure that your expectations for your travels are in line with the culture of the hostel.

you choose. If you're looking for a tranquil serene getaway, don't be at a hotel that offers an open bar and dance floor and reverse.

For accommodation you have the best choices for finding free or affordable lodging. However, I highly recommend that you think about using free accommodations as even if the location you're staying at is $10 per night (not uncommon) If you're going in vacation for 10 days this is $100 that could have been saved with Couchsurfing. If you're struggling Free is always the best option.

Chapter 6: Food And Activities

In terms of eating out and other activities when travelling, you're likely need to pay for it that's the truth. this, and the earlier you accept this fact the more advantageous. As an overall rule of thumb I suggest that you pick the option you value most to you and then spend your the money you can afford there. It doesn't mean you shouldn't spend any amount on any other (obviously that's just not possible) It's just that you must determine the priorities you place on and then plan your spending according to. For instance I'm not foodie, but I've had scrambled egg and spaghetti (both cheap and quick meals) for several days in a row. I've had scrambled eggs for breakfast, and pasta with a cheap sauce from the supermarket for dinner and lunch. There are foodies who are shocked at the idea of this but here it is. When I ate inexpensive food and then cooking the food on my Couchsurfing host's home or in a the hostel I was able to spend my money on excursions and events that I was more attracted. In contrast, if you're passionate about trying local cuisine it's the one you should allocate the majority of your cash into.

When you've decided which is most important to you, then you can follow the tips below to cut costs on both of them to ensure that, even though you know the area you'd like to reduce costs on yet you're still saving money than someone who's not as knowledgeable.

Food

1.) Have a larger lunch and then a smaller dinner. In the US most likely, you were raised to eat your biggest meal of the day towards the time each day. If you're travelling, I would suggest that you eat your main meal during lunchtime. This isn't some kind of "it's healthier for you nonsense" ... keep in mind that this book is about conserving money, not to help you to maintain a healthy eating plan It's true that I eat more than a human would. If you have a huge meal at lunch, two things happen 1.) There's more food than you're able to eat and you'll have leftovers to eat dinner when you're hungry and save money when you need to buy an additional dinner after lunch. 2.) You'll finish the meal and, since it's a larger meal than you're used,

you stay fuller for longer. When you're starving and again, it's way too late in the evening to eat a full meal and so you have to eat smaller portions to keep your stomach until breakfast. So, you don't have to buy the whole meal. It's probably only a small amount of food, that's less expensive and will save your money. If none of these occur, then either you're not eating a large enough meal or you are a gluttonous eater In this case, I'd suggest that keep snacks in your bag every moment of the day to ensure you can save money by not purchasing big meals two times a day and instead grabbing snacks throughout the day (snacks are more affordable as compared to meals). This leads me to my next tip...

2.) No matter what your appetite, it is recommended to take at least a small snack with your person to ensure you don't allow your hunger to get so bad enough to make you eat the first food you see regardless of cost. If you're starving enough, your budget will be blown out the of the window and all you'll be thinking about eating. It's likely that you'll take the fastest route and the best option will be returning to the spot you are staying to cook yourself an inexpensive food item that is within your budget. It's likely that you'll find yourself in an expensive restaurant that focuses on tourists, with all menus available in English and where the staff members are fluent in English.

If you're hungry, you don't thinking about value or price but food, so you should be prepared for it.

3.) Be sure that the accommodation you are staying in has kitchen facilities that you are able to use so that are able to cook meals on your own. This is the most affordable alternative regardless of where you live. It's no surprise that at home, grabbing groceries and cooking food is less expensive than dining out for every meal. This is the same everywhere in the world. But, even if aren't staying in a place with an kitchen, you can visit the local grocery stores. Sometimes , they'll have pizzas and sandwiches less than the cost of a meal in a restaurant, and they're sufficient to last for at least two hours. You can also buy fresh fruit in grocery stores and it's a low-cost and tasty snack, particularly when you're desire of something sweet.

4.) If you choose to take a meal out, make sure you don't fall into tourist traps. Finding a restaurant where the employees working there are fluent in English while the menu itself is written in English is simple and easy however, you'll have to pay for that convenience. Be adventurous and explore where locals go. Visit a restaurant where the menu doesn't appear in English and you may need to bring a menu

You can tell the waiters tell them what you'd like. I've performed this gesture in more countries than I could count, and have never been served food that was so unpalatable that I felt as if I had wasted my money (but keep in mind that I'm not an eater, so I'm not particularly picky when it is about food). If you're a person with restricted diets or know that you're picky eaters, this could be more difficult your way, yet not difficult. Nearly everyone has an iPhone or a smartphone and the best thing to do is install google translate. Google translate app, and make certain that you are using your language in the nation you're planning to download before getting there to utilize the app to make translations of menus in offline. If you're a bit adventurous I'm going to tell you that it's a lot more enjoyable playing Foreign Menu Roulette.

a. A. Side tip A. Side tip: If you're staying at an accommodation, homestay or hostel, or Couchsurfing it's possible to ask your host or proprietor of the hostel where you can find cheap and delicious food. If you're a vegetarian, or have other restrictions, they'll likely be able to direct you to the right place because they're locals and familiar with the area.

b. Another suggestion: If you go to an establishment (in an area where drinking water from the tap is of a safe quality) ensure that you request table or tap water. It's a common usage across the US to promptly bring complimentary drinking water for the tables. In other countries, they will serve you bottles of water and charge you for it.

5.) Be prepared to try street food! Street food is definitely one of my most memorable travel experiences. Although it may look unappetizing, but the majority of the time , it's good and is always inexpensive because it's what locals consume. If you decide to eat street food I suggest that you drink a cola along with your meal to prevent stomach-related issues. This isn't proven by science, however I've used it in every country all the way from Thailand all the way to Cuba and it has always proved to be effective for me. Test it out and check it out. If not, think about bringing a stomach pain medication to take with you, like Pepto-Bismol as having diarrhea just once in a while is certainly worth it to eat street food as I mentioned, it's delicious and affordable and if you're in a pinch, it's hard to argue with this reasoning.

6) If you're planning to enjoy a night out with friends like you do at home, prepare for the game with a bottle of alcohol from the grocery store. It's obvious that alcohol consumed in bars and clubs is more costly. Like you would at home, you can save some cash and prepare for the game with cheap alcohol that you purchase

yourself. (I've even experienced Couchsurfing hosts who played with me and drank alcohol with me and I didn't have to purchase alcohol prior to the game... and no, this wasn't due to being an attractive girl, it's an experience that's just part of being a part of the

Couchsurfing encounter.) But let's get real for a moment. If you're a woman probably won't need to purchase your beverages at the bar and it's your choice whether or not you'd like to purchase the pregame liquor.11

Activities

1.) Bring your student ID with you. Really, bring it along take it with you. It's impossible to predict whether something will include discounts for students. I've received discounts for students on everything from toursto admission fees to castles museums, and even Ice cream. Bring it along. Even though sometimes the folks responsible for applying the discount will offer it to you if are young enough and sound convincing but sometimes they'll want evidence. It's practically free to take it along and can help you save money on things you'd like to accomplish. In truth I've been out of college for the past one and a half years, however, I have retained my ID from college for this exact reason. I continue to utilize it to obtain discounts for students whenever I am able to. I'm young, so I'm not required to convince anyone that I'm still a student. However, I'm likely to keep it in my bag and use it until it's not working any more and there's no way for me to pretend to be a college student.

2.) If you're looking for museums or galleries of art, you should look into the city that you're planning to visit has free day at the museum and whether or not it matches to your plans for travel. It's likely to be a bit more crowded during that time however, you'll still be able to access the museum for free. If you're female and traveling by yourself, I would recommend being extra cautious when going out in the evening. To be honest I've traveled on my own for the past five years and have never felt that it's worth the risk of going in a club or nightclub in a foreign city entirely on my own. Join the help of your Couchsurfing host, or meet a few guests at your hotel and meet up with in a group, or look to Facebook to check if there are other female travellers who are solo within the same city you, who are looking to an evening out. It is true that this book is supposed to focus on money, not security but as a woman, I truly am concerned about the safety of fellow women who travel alone.

And you have the chance to go to the same places that you'd see in the day you paid for.

3.) If you're considering something that you could only complete without a professional guide, for reasons beyond your control, don't accept the first price you're offered. Even if you're able to negotiate to lower the cost, make sure you inquire about other options. They might be able to offer better value and can meet their cost.

Perhaps another tour operator is just $5 more costly, however it comes with food and a tour guide with 3or more decades of expertise. When you're paying for tours, though it can be difficult if in a financial bind, you should always consider the value over cost. This will make a huge difference in the experience. In general, don't choose the first deal you receive. Do some research. Visit different tour operators and inquire about their rates and make sure you inquire about what's included in the price to be sure you understand exactly what you're getting for your money.

a. A. Side note After you've browsed around, do not purchase until you've checked on the internet. Sometimes it's more affordable to book in person when you're located in the country. However, often it's more affordable when you book on the internet. You should check both ways to ensure that you're getting the most value for money. Additionally, certain tour operators use contractors as guides, which means that they pay guides to accompany the guests they (the tour companies) discover. If this is the case you'll always be paying more as the tour company has to earn money from each individual in addition to paying for the guide's fees. So, it's always better to directly book an experienced guide, if you are able to as this eliminates the middleman and means you pay an amount between $10 and $30 less.

4.) Make use of the free walking tours like Sandeman's. They're available in many major cities, and even if they're not located in your city that you're visiting, an alternative company is.

It's never hurts to take a take a look. It has made the process of figuring things out from other countries so much simpler, and it's a shame not to take advantage of it. You can enter the following keywords into the Google query: (city/country name here) and free activities to enjoy.

5.) The majority of people aren't aware that you can purchase tickets to a single show in the last minute. That means if you're planning to attend an opera, ballet, play, and so on. The chances are that you'll be able to purchase a single ticket for a bargain on the day before, or even before the performance (obviously this is only for you're travelling on your own). The reason that these seats are so inexpensive is that they are

It's because some people have purchased tickets in a way that there's a spot in an audience which the venue recognizes is difficult to sell since most people don't go to shows on their own. The seats are discounted significantly in hopes of convincing people to purchase them, regardless of knowing that they'll not be able to share a seat with the person they are familiar with. Take a second to think about it that the show is going to continue regardless, so it's smart business sense to make sure the venue does everything it can to market every seat. Even if your seat is awful and has a view that isn't clear but who's to say that you shouldn't get an even better, more spacious seat when intermission begins. I've been there and no one cares. Keep an eye out for these seats during the event and ensure that they aren't empty.

Chapter 7: Haggling

You might be thinking why I've committed an entire chapter on haggling. What if I could have said that it's beneficial to bargain and aid you in getting an even better deal and get finished with the whole thing? Yes however, the main purpose of this book is to offer those who are broken as a joke the best advice to make travel more low costs. What's more? haggling could reduce your spending by half in the countries that are known to be bargaining (which are usually the most affordable countries to visit and therefore, ones that which you should visit even if you're not financially stable).

I do not know about you however, being a child in the US I didn't have any experience of haggling prior to the time I began traveling. Due to this, I was gypped more times than I can remember and especially when I first began traveling it was money I didn't have the money to waste. To give you an example of how you can take a lesson from my mistakes:

My first visit to Thailand at the age of 19 , I began looking for a bus to transport the journey to Bangkok until the crossing of the ferry to Koh Chang. Koh Chang. I believed I had found the best price at $10 since I was basing my notion of a reasonable price on my understanding about US and UK costs. Rooky move. I hopped on the bus and asked other passengers about the amount they'd paid. There was no one who had paid the same amount as me. One person had paid $2 for the ride. I was a fool and I would never want to see this occur to you. This is why I don't say that you should negotiate and I'd like to provide you with the tools needed to be able to bargain effectively.

Haggling goes beyond an exchange of counter-offers and a sense of the value of an item worth to you as well as what it's worth to the person selling it. Both depend on the specific circumstances. For instance, a shop owner may consider an item to be less valuable at the final day, just to make a profit. On the other hand, you may consider an item to be more valuable if you are certain that it's unique or triggers emotions within your. Being aware of where each individual (including you) is on the same page is essential to bargaining.

Here are my suggestions for negotiate the cost of an item:

1.) Look around the area. Do not enter the first shop you come across Find an item you like and then begin to bargain. In this case you don't have any or any of these cards. You don't know which stores offer the same or similar items, so you could consider the item to be worth over what the value. Visit different stores or look at other stalls in the vicinity of the location you purchased the item to determine whether it's a common product.

2.) Don't be overly obvious. It is best to not touch the product until you're ready to bargain to ensure that the seller isn't able to tell the item you're interested in. If you fall into the trap of taking a closer look at the item carefully and the seller comes up and begins discussing the item then simply take the item off the table or walk away and claim that you just wanted to look. The act of haggling is deceitful. If you are clearly interested in the product and are willing to declare that you are interested in the item the seller will know that you'll be likely to purchase regardless of what price they offer you (as as long as it's not too expensive) and you won't be able haggle as much due to this. Don't be concerned whether you leave empty handed.

3.) It depends on the item or service. Haggling can be similar to those pick-your-own adventure novels that were very popular in the 90s, you know, those books where the plot would take a different turn according to your choices. It's as that: The way you negotiate will depend on whether the product you're looking for is rare or common.

a. Be aware that "hand-made" does not have anything to determine whether an item is rare or common particularly in countries with lower prices. This is the reason step 1 is crucial. When the product is popular and lots of vendors are selling it you'll be able negotiate prices that are much less than when the item is rare and not many other sellers sell it. For instance in Central America hand-woven bags and wallets that are brightly colored are a hugely popular souvenir. But, even though they're handmade they are sold by everyone. They're on sale in the streets and in shops, and at the markets, and everywhere else. Since they're everywhere and sellers face a lot of competition, you'll have an advantage when you negotiate the price you'd like to pay. If the price is lower, you can negotiate.

It's more common, and harder to come across, you could bargain, however it's unlikely you'll be successful in obtaining a substantial reduction from the price you were offered.

However in the world of bargaining, knowing is always the best tool.

Also, before you leave: find out whether the product is available everywhere or exclusively at one store.

4.) No matter if the item you're looking to purchase is expensive, uncommon, or even cheap it is always a good idea to attempt to get the seller to counteroffer the first time to the original offer. You've just have read that paragraph and you're thinking "Who would ever consider counteroffering an offer they've made? The seller wouldn't even think about this, you're insane!" But I swear I'm not. If you can convince the seller to make a counteroffer to their own offer first, you're exactly where you're supposed to be in because the seller laid out their cards on the table. seller is more concerned about the sale as a whole than the amount he'll get out of the deal.

Keep in mind that the more you are aware of the events that take place while you're bargaining the easier it is to bargain - so be attentive to the smallest things.

a. Once you've realized it's possible to do it, you have to figure out how to do it "how." What can you convince the seller to counteroffer your own offer? One method I've discovered works extremely my experience is to go to the object (or in the case of a large item you can point it directly at it) and then inquire about how much it costs. At this point, you're telling the seller you are interested in what you're selling, and he'll be delighted by the prospect of selling the item. It is important to leverage this enthusiasm against them. Right following (And I'm referring to this.

Don't stop and pretend to think about the item, do not look back at the item and then think about the price he offered you. If the above.) If he or she offers you a price, and you have to place the item in the trash or take it off your hands and look shocked (don't overdo it) and claim that this is a lot of money. It is true that in the space of just an hour, the person selling has gone from believing that he/she's likely to sell to thinking that he/she will not. The excitement felt by the seller could be used against them and 9 times out of 10 sellers will say something like "It's typically that amount and I'll offer a discount.

You pay only ___ dollars." The seller has counteroffered his own offer

And it is now time to haggle. begins.12

5.) Find out what you're after. Before you make your counter offer it is important to know what you're willing to spend for this item as well as what you're willing to accept if you are pressured (i.e. be aware of your minimum and maximum). If you don't know what an item will cost you then you aren't capable of haggling effectively. If, for instance, I was offered an item that I wanted to purchase for $30 , and the seller counters with $25, I'd attempt to negotiate the price down to $15 but the maximum I'd willing to purchase it for is $17. It's about 50% less and this is why saying that bargaining could reduce your expenses by half. It can be done with souvenirs, food items (depending on the location) as well as excursions and other activities. Learning to bargain can be a huge savings for those who are financially strapped but still wants to travel the world.

6.) Counteroffer, knowing that the haggling will go on. Sellers are very unlikely to accept the first counteroffer you offer (and when they do, it's likely that you didn't bargain far enough and could have received a lower rate). This is why the step 5 is crucial when you don't know the amount you'd like to purchase the product, you'll never have a good idea of what your counteroffer ought to be. In the same way, if you consider an item that's initial offer was $30, and the counteroffer of the seller was $25, if I'm looking to purchase the item for $15, I'm likely to counteroffer a lower amount than $15 to ensure that I have the the opportunity to negotiate. I'm aware that $8 is a ridiculous price for the item and sellers will think that as well, however I'll make an $8 counteroffer in order to bargain my way until $15 (the price I was hoping to pay for it all through). After I have made my absurdly low counteroffer, it's time for the seller to be astonished and claim that selling the item to you at that price would be the same as offering it to anyone for free. That's how the game plays out. It's one astonished "No you can't be able to" one after the other until you reach you get a 12. Remember that this is crucial since it gives you an advantage (and when you're in negotiations you must always have the upper hand). The seller has just stated the reason why he/she is seeking is a sale. So, you're able to bargain with the goal of paying the lowest amount the seller is willing to pay since you are aware that in the end, they need to sell.

A reasonable price is set.

7.) Don't do to others what they did to you. The haggling will keep going and you should follow the seller about the amount you are supposed to increase with every counteroffer. For instance, if a seller in the previous example offers $20 after the counteroffer of $8 you will know that the seller is WAAAAYYYY

The price was exaggerated for the product (because the counteroffers are dropping many times).

In this scenario, you must make the exact opposite. You should counteroffer just $1 or $2 for each $5. In this case it's very likely to purchase the item for less than you originally thought of. If, however, the seller from the above example counteroffers you $23, you have to increase the price by more (not excessively however, still greater than the seller in the act of good-faith). His counteroffer's low value lets you know that at the very least, he believes the price he's set for his item is just a bit over a fair price, and they don't believe it's worth less. Since he is of this opinion (as evident by his ridiculously modest counteroffer) you have to prove that you're willing with them that the item is worth more than you originally thought. The counteroffer you make this time must be between $11 and $13.

(continuing in the same scenario). This is why it is important to keep a maximum number in your head. In this instance it is much harder to reach the sweet spot of $15 (not impossible, but certainly more challenging). After the counteroffer is a good faith one You should only increase by not more than $2 per time until a deal is reached. You must be respectful to the seller's conviction in the reasonable price however, you don't want to appear to be being a swindler.

8.) If you are able to make a counteroffer to the amount you're prepared to settle, you must stand your stand. Be aware that in most situation it is the last counteroffer. You've decided you're happy with the amount you're ready to spend for this product. If the seller attempts to offer you a higher price prices, you need to be assertive and inform them that you're only looking to purchase the product for $15. The seller could appear annoyed or even claim they will sell it for less than $15

It's like giving you the product. Whatever he or she tells you, be firm 90% of the time , they'll concede since at the end, they would like to sell the item.

a. However that for the remaining 10 percent of the time when you truly need this particular item, counteroffer it just 1 more times. In the case above I'd offer $16 as my final price because it's just one additional dollar, but less than what I'm willing to pay.

9) You'll be happy in the knowledge that you've made yourself money, and you still achieved what you desired. This is because that's what the way of life revolves around.

Chapter 8: Work Options Abroad

This section is for those among you wanting to travel but don't want to travel for the long haul.

The recommendations I offer in this chapter may not be intended for all people. If you are easily homesick or have difficulty getting over culture shock after moving from a large city to a small city or vice versa may want to skip this chapter. It's not because I want you to leave your comfort zone to try something completely new. Actually this is exactly what I hope for in this book. Instead, I'd like to ensure that the farms, hostels and families that you could be working for feel disappointed when the person they relied on for a specific length of time departed early due to missing the return home. If you're not naturally a gambler and enjoy being in difficult and uncomfortable situations, I would suggest making a couple of short excursions first.

As I left for the United States at first, I travelled for a whole year. I completed two semesters of studying abroad and also spent the winter holiday in Thailand. However, I realize the fact that this degree of commitment to the unknown isn't for everyone, and that's why this section is the final one. I hope that you be equipped with the tools that you require to travel affordable prices so that you can start planning the adventures you've always dreamed of going on. I'll also present to you the concept of traveling as a way to earn money (and not only as something to invest your money in).

However, I'm also incorporating the possibility of volunteering in this section, since you're basically working in another country, and are provided with free accommodation and occasionally food items.

It's still technically a matter of getting money, but that it's in money. Volunteering abroad can drastically lower your costs for travel and you don't have to spend nearly as much before you travel for a long time, making long-term travel more affordable and less burdensome financially. This is why Here are all the ways you can volunteer abroad to make your travel less expensive and something that you can manage sustainably even as a poordollar Student at college.

1.) Volunteer for a local group (lionsclub.org, optimist.org, rotary.org) for example. There are many organizations near your area that you could be a volunteer for abroad.

Numerous companies within the US go to different countries on a regular basis to

Aid in the cause. These are usually third-world countries, which are known to be the most affordable and, since you're with a reputable organization, you could also raise funds to go on your trip (I believe you can do that but it's odd to ask someone else to help you fund your spring break trip in Cancun). If you're looking to travel in an evident, meaningful manner it's possible to think about this kind of volunteer work.13

2.) Farmstays (such such as wwoof.org as well as anyworkanywhere.com) is a. These aren't suitable for all. For instance, I've yet to take part in an agricultural stay (although I've considered it). Farmstays are exactly what it is: you get to stay at the farm for free and possibly even meals for free as a reward for doing farm work. This could mean whatever you want, depending on the kind or farm it is you'll be staying at. It could involve picking fruit and taking care of livestock and riding a tractor and so on. You're likely to do the work for the benefit of lodging and meals. I know friends who've done this specifically in Australia and they enjoyed the experience and described it as an interesting method of learning the new skills (not to mention the fact that physical labor meant that a lot of them ended up in quite good shape during their stay on the farm).

3.) Hostel jobs in hostels (hostelworld.com and backpack.co.nz for instance) are a. In the event that you "work" in a hostel the duties you perform can be very different dependent on the hostel. This is an excellent method to swap work in exchange for a room at no cost and perhaps even free meals (depending on the amount of food those who stay in the hostel have left behind). I've put "work" in quotation marks since you'll want to be payed. I know, that sounds weird, but trust me you're going to want to not receive 13 You can also travel for charity through organizations such as globaladventurechallenges.com, acrossthedivide.com and charitytreks.com - these are similar to, for example, running a 5k for charity, but they involve traveling to another location to participate in a charity event (running, hiking, cycling, etc.). This is another method to ensure that your trips have an immediate, positive impact on the society.

The payment is in the form of monetary compensation for the job that you do in the hostel, mostly due to visa issues. So long as there is no money is exchanged, transferring your labor to get room and board is a fantastic method to avoid having to obtain a work visa to work in a different country. Some countries have work visas that can be extremely difficult to obtain, particularly for Americans. If you're not earning or anything else, you're technically not employed by the government, so you're not required to have to obtain a work visa. A hostel could be a better choice for those who don't want to invest in the quantity of physical work required for working on farms.

4) Workaway.info

a. Another website on which you can search for "work" overseas (there is a requirement to pay a once-off registration fee). The reason I chose to include this site by itself is that it's a sort of grab-bag of positions and jobs. It's impossible to know what you're likely to discover. A quick search on the site shows that there are a variety of places to volunteer as well as some farms. There are babysitters' positions to be found. It's one of my top websites to visit because there is no telling what you might find. I recently spoke with a lady from Norway who shared with me that once to have fun she checked out the jobs available in her country. She found there were three people who decided to go sailing towards the shores of Italy and to island travel across Greece were posting that they could accommodate an additional passenger in the event that that person would be willing to volunteer and contribute food. What a bizarre extraordinary experience. The website is certainly worth a look If you're looking to exchange your expertise for a free room and board anywhere in the world. You could also have an opportunity to master something new.

These are my recommendations in the case of technically "unpaid" work. There is no monetary reward for the work you perform through these alternatives, however, you'll get a sleeping space and even meals (which are a large portion of the expenses associated with travel). If you aren't content with just traveling on a budget, but earn money while traveling, these ideas are perfect suitable for you.

You can:

5.) Participate in the role of an Au Pair (greataupair.com and aupair.com)

a. If you're a lover of having children around, you could take a break during the summer (or all whole year) being an au pair. While it's the most sought-after job in Europe but I've also noticed jobs being advertised across other continents too (there aren't as many jobs available). The responsibilities of an au pair will differ considerably based on your family and the contract you sign. There are families that will help you travel to Europe and give you their private apartment and also give an extra amount for food in addition to your agreed upon wage. Some families will only provide the use of an extra space in their home, as well as a place at their table each meal. Some families might ask that you take care of the kids all day long while some may need you to spend 3 to 5 hours playing with their children and talking English with them. It's all about the family you'll end up working for. However, this is determined before you even leave home and you must be aware about what family members wants from you prior to when you go.14

6) Jobs that are seasonal available in Australia (goworkabout.com)

a. There's a reason why Australia has always been about foreign workers. It's perhaps one of the most simple nations to find work and also get a work permit around the globe. This site lists all kinds of jobs from babysitter to chef depending on the skills you have.

As the au pair you are payed for the work you perform and, yes, you require a visa as a result of it. This website assists you with your visa forms, tax documents as well as insurance for travel and bank account applications, and just about everything else you might need assistance in relocating into Australia in order to start your new job. If an English-speaking nation close to Indonesia is your ideal of the ideal place to spend a few months or even a year, this could be the ideal choice for you.

14 It's easier for women to be employed as au pairs than men, however don't get discouraged. There are men who are au pairs, but you may have to search a bit harder.

7) Remote work (weworkremotely.com, flexjobs.com, workingnomads.co, etc.) A. I didn't land an online job until after I graduated, but it doesn't mean that you can't be better than me and secure one when you're studying at the moment. If you're averse to any type of technological or social media abilities then this could be an easy task for you. I do not but it did take me a long time to find a job someone with an English major could perform from their laptop.

If you're determined you can do anything. This is the ideal alternative as working remotely, the work you do isn't location-specific and you can work wherever you'd like at any time. This is something that you could continue to do after college, and you never know? You might just never stop exploring and join the ranks of digital nomads that call this world home.

I'd like to stress that these are just very few ideas to find jobs in the world.

One thing I highly suggest is that if are aware of where you want to travel to, determine what abilities you possess that you could be paid for, then you begin Google to find out more.

In the course of my college years, I was aware that I wanted to return to Europe to spend the summer. I knew that I would not have enough money to cover the cost I also knew that I had worked with children. I began searching for English teaching jobs , summer camp positions, etc. I was offered a job at a camp for summer located in the Swiss alps. I applied and was selected as a counselor. I did not actually be a counselor at camp however, as the camp was canceled because of low enrollment. I was not discouraged, however. I reconnected with my online account and found work for an Au pairing located in Corsica, France only 2 weeks after. I still had the chance to spend this summer traveling around Europe as I had hoped and learned that it's never too late to devise an alternative plan.

If you are really looking to get a job in another country:

1.) Be aware of where you would like to be (roughly).

2.) Be aware of what you're skilled at.

3.) Explore the web (you are incredibly proficient in using keywords when you do Google search results).

Chapter 9: Truth Of Saving Money

The reality about finances is that they're always a finite resource, however, the limits vary between people. The issue with traveling cheaply that I noticed missing in my own research but is that there are times when you're looking to save as you can on specific aspects of your trip that can be applied to another portion of the trip.

In fact, one my first experiences while trying to find ways to cut my expenses was from a man who claimed that anything other than a airfare to get there was a waste of money explaining the ways to get food and even sleep on floors if you did it without spending a cent.

While this is technically an option, it's certainly not something that the majority of people are comfortable with This guide is mostly focused on traveling with a certain level of comfort, which that you choose according to your budget and personal preference.

It could be that you fly with RyanAir which allows you to stay in a five star hotel, or perhaps it's living in hostels in order to pay for the luxury train journey. However, you'll want to find the most value for what you're doing. That's the premise of this guide. A complete analysis of all the alternatives, and how to save money (versus the amount of time it appears savings) on any of these options, based on my own experiences.

One thing I discovered during the process was that the majority of the advice was applicable to more expensive travel like high-end hotels, or perhaps the dream first class flight!

The Most Important Lesson

The reason for a lot of this guide will turn out to be single word that is flexibility. Always be flexibleand consider the many aspects of travel as you are able to. While your travel dates may not be easily altered consider accepting the possibility of a different day or alternative method of travel generally speaking, the travel industry is looking for those who will utilize their space and make the most of people who have to be there at certain times. the majority of these travelers are business travelers that aren't cost-conscious, however the information in this guide you are likely to be.

For a concrete illustration of that, travel between London and Paris If you purchase just a few days prior the trip, from between Monday and Friday, will cost you about PS258 via train or PS300+ via plane. If you purchase two months in advance and travel from Wednesday until the weekend, then exactly the same trip, sitting next to the person who purchased tickets that are expensive and costs PS29 per way via train, or PS40 on the plane.

The reasoning behind it is the fact that traveling is demand-driven business that sells items based on what you're willing pay, not on the basis of the amount they cost to make. It sounds like something that isn't so, but in reality, it allows business travelers to pay morewhile also finding an opportunity to offer people who will pay less to do thus, ensuring that the company is able to earn a profit. The same principle applies in various ways to hotels, buses, and theme parks!

This is why I can travel to anywhere from 5-10 countries each year. Because I can be flexible with my working hours, I can enjoy many months, most destinations, and even the majority of locations for departure. I realize that this may not be the case for all people however there are numerous other ways to save money , however should you wish to enhance the amount of traveling you make by an number of times and you are looking for flexibility, flexibility can aid you!

What Don't Work

In the effort to market affiliates or advertising there are many things websites and videos say are beneficial and can save you huge amounts of money. Let's explore the things you need to know about first.

The price of tickets in the privacy of your browser There's a widely circulated story that airlines make use of cookies to record what you did when you browsed the price of a flight, so they know when you'll be back at the identical flights. Human psychology can suggests that you're already committing to purchase when you go back to the same product. But with airlines, this isn't to be the case. Because prices can rise even when using third party sites, or even when cookies are turned off If it's true they're tracking the interest of flights, but not the interest on the trip. What it can teach, however, is that prices increase much more frequently than they fall and fluctuate on a daily basis.

Tickets purchased in another country is not a problem. With a handful of exceptions using the VPN or changing your computer's location to make it appear like you're in another won't make you pay less for flights. Although airlines make distinctions according to route, connection or other factors, they typically don't do it depending on the location of your destination or currency therefore, don't invest $50 for an VPN with the hope of getting huge savings on your flights. However, they are beneficial when you travel as well as for saving money on other things.

Dressing well and soliciting an upgrade This advice is recited in the media every time the subject of upgrade on flights comes up, however it's not been the case for quite some time, in fact, if it ever was even. Recently, there were a few fires at some airlines due to employees having made their own decisions about upgrades rather than making use of the method (which is based on a range of factors including how much you'd like to travel in first class being not one of the criteria).

Airlines sell these upgrades at massive prices, and many people purchase them . Why should you expect them to be no cost? Also, a suit or extravagant clothing is not likely to make your flight more pleasant, but will be a health risk during long flights.

Picking Your Transport

The air travel isn't the only method of getting from point to the destination, and while it is usually the fastest however, it's not always the most relaxing. The thought of putting yourself inside a tube and being tossed around for hours isn't for everyone, when you add the stress of arriving at the airport before the scheduled time and the stress airlines put you through and more, it can be a great time to catch trains or buses.

In general, if you don't see anything else in this article trains may be less expensive but the price is usually a greater cost for a longer, but also more pleasant and easy journey. There are numerous exceptions we'll discuss; however, be prepared that when you book your trip, you'll pay the same amount for planes and trains.

Buses tend to be less romantic, dull and slow. They are however an affordable option for getting from one location. They could be substituted by buses that run for 8 hours, however they can be rented at a bargain price, and the destinations are extremely adaptable because of their utilization of the road network instead of train runways or tracks. It is cheaper than driving on your own however not as quick.

Legacy Carriers

Legacy or full-fare carriers are generally in existence because they've always existed, and often in the form of competitions with prices 60 to 70% less. For someone who began traveling following the acceptance of the budget equivalents and budget equivalents, I am baffled that people pay extra to utilize these types of fares.

Although I frequently have to use these for the majority of long haul flights as well as specifically for short haul flights. Here is a look at the mess of price of tickets. While there are some specific to a particular country, these are not the only ones but they will apply to any airline:

Take a return flight whenever feasible - As these companies tend to increase the cost of flights shorter than a specified length, they charge extremely high minimum rates for single tickets in general. That means that you'll usually receive return tickets for less than one ticket, which implies that tickets for single trips are typically not worth it even for a one-time flight.

For instance an example, a round trip ticket of London to Argentina costs around $900 if purchased in advance for a month. What is the price for a single cost?

Return to the same city that you flew to Similar to the one above, many methods will consider that an "open jaw" ticket as not an return ticket, but rather two singles. Be sure to check carefully, as under certain circumstances this can be acceptable but at least , you need to use an identical airport on the return trip.

At the minimum it is generally recommended. This is the reason I was able to get a ticket from Zurich to Geneva traveling through Canada.

Always make sure to check single tickets just in case The most interesting part is that most airlines view this as a concern too and will therefore set the minimum price for single tickets reasonable, allowing passengers to avoid the price of return tickets by purchasing 2 single tickets for the identical flights!

Fly indirect - This could be where your pricing goes extremely absurd, since numerous airlines make you pay more for directly. It sounds like a good idea, since it's a superior service but taking a flight between London up to Dubai is a lot more expensive than traveling from Paris all the way to London and returning to Dubai regardless of being the London to Dubai part of the journey using the same aircraft, operated by an airline that is the exact same.

The savings could be enough to justification the cost of a second flight to Paris or maybe staying a night in Paris. The airports with the lowest prices differ between countries and yet, it is interesting that changing the source of your flight to go through an indirect route will help you save money and also earn you greater airline miles.

Take a break from the journey. An absurd case can be London to Bangkok with the option of stopping in Dubai will cost less than the tickets for London through Dubai.

This is due to what's commonly referred to as premium pricing since both cities are rich, including business travelers who will pay whatever price is stated, while Bangkok is typically visited by tourists. If you're flying on an one-way ticket it's not a problem that you from "accidently" not making the second flight and earning the enormous savings.

Make Advance Bookings The fundamental idea behind pre-booking is one I won't have for anyone who reads this article but the idea that it's always best to make reservations earlier isn't necessarily the case. Many airlines offer tickets to sell one year prior to when they depart and the prices fluctuate many times prior to the time.

It's difficult to discern any significant information by looking at it. So here's the average over all of the year for every region, assuming that the starting or ending date is Europe.

The Destination Cheapest Standard Booking Time

North America 2 weeks

Central America 3 months

Africa 2 months

Asia 6 months

Caribbean 4 Months of Caribbean

Europe 2 to 3 weeks in Europe

South America 5 months

Middle East 5 months

South Pacific 3 months

Even even if your flight doesn't start or finishing in Europe This will provide you with a rough idea of 3 months being nearly always the perfect time to travel and with lesser time for shorter flights, and more time for longer ones.

If you're interested in exploring and are flexible on the destination you're interested in There are usually great last-minute deals to be found particularly for countries that require visas or visa waivers. This is the reason for some of the $99 transatlantic flights I've experienced!

Make use of the loyalty program In the case of a few exceptions, every major airline with full service has a loyalty program that caters to frequent travellers. Although you may not consider your self as being a regular traveler however, by enrolling in one of these programs, you'll reap some advantages. For example, you're less likely to get kicked off the plane. Even just flying once every year will eventually earn you enough points to redeem anything even if it's the chance to save on another flight. If you don't sign up, you're taking a chance to lose the opportunity to earn a cash back of 2-20% possibility!

Demand-based pricing - The airlines set their prices the price based on the amount they think you're willing to pay, not on their cost or any other factor. This means that trying to determine the most unattractive dates to fly will yield excellent results.

This is also the reason why flying to Bulgaria is more affordable that flying to London or the reason why Wednesdays and Tuesdays are usually so cheap and not a day that vacation or business travelers would like to take advantage of this time of year, or to travel to the day to reach their destination.

Make sure you check the prices regularly - The reality of so many incredible bargains - such as the $47 round-trip transatlantic flight (I have also had the pleasure of having the pleasure of) can be found in the fact that they usually occur by accident or during flash sales. The difference between these two is difficult to discern however, setting up an email tracker that emails you each day can do. Or, you could frequently check airfare prices to ensure that you are getting a fair price when it is revealed!

Budget Airlines

It is essential to travel by air in nearly every trip anywhere you'd think of "travelling" and is often the most costly element of any trip even though it is the least enjoyable. In spite of that there are still many who choose to fly with an airline that is in line with their nation, or because they are afraid of what the lower end of the scale actually is as. Both are not a good option for an experience that which you're probably not going to enjoy.

In reality, budget airlines are less efficient than regular airlines in many ways. You will likely to experience a less packed plane, and slightly less service. If you think the fact that they cost 10x less implies that they're skimping on security or basic services however, it's usually not the scenario. Indeed, many budget airlines are placed higher than their more costly counterparts as well as AirAsia is one of the top ranked airlines in the world in spite of being "budget".

The main reason they are able to provide tickets for such low prices, however it has to do with the concept of a packed plane. In contrast to a traditional airline that seeks to sell tickets and earn profits on every ticket however, a budget airline will have no profits on the first 85 percent of tickets purchased on an airplane. But, by filling each seat and earning profits through you, they could make sure they cover their costs and also be able to earn profits on the last few seats which they can sell at a price that is much more expensive.

They also have lower costssince they drop off at times when they can get lower landing slots, they don't pay commission to other websites when ticket booking, and their employees do not have to sign those union agreements as the major airline companies are. They usually do not offer connecting flights at prices that are cheaper than one-way and will not leave their planes in the air for too long in a row.

A Norwegian dreamliner in the air for only one quick spin before heading off again for a flight later in the next day.

These factors together with the large number of hours that a budget airline has to spend in the air, actually gives them the newest and most modern aircrafts. Norwegian is the only airline to fly 787's from London as well as Ryanair is the only airline to fly exclusively brand new 737's because the cost of fuel is lower. This works to your advantage!

The real challenge with low-cost airlines is to make sure that you're among the passengers who can afford the cheapest ticket and not those who make profits made from the tickets (on identical routes, on the exact same day on RyanAir I've paid PS9 and PS200 It doesn't require the brains of a genius to determine the price you'd prefer to pay)

Despite the lowest rates in Europe that are filled to capacity on all of their seats and having low overhead expenses is what makes ryanair among the top airlines around the globe!

The most crucial thing to keep in mind is that the majority of these airlines earn money through secondary revenue sources. When you purchase your ticket, there are usually a number of extras that you can add on, but it's best to stay clear of this (Because you'll not be able to profit from the suggestions earlier in the guide) You'll never find a better or even a comparable bargain by doing this!

Other Types of Transport

So, based on where you're located there's a good chance that one or both of these options is accessible to you. In certain cities, trains aren't an option (certain islands and larger countries such as Australia only have a couple trains or no lines) and in certain countries, buses are not permitted to service intercity routes in the nation, like Sweden where buses are permitted to serve a single stop in the country due to of the laws governing competition with

Trains

Trains are a relaxing and simple way to get from one location to the next and remove a lot of stress from flying and generally transporting passengers from the center to center. While most countries offer at least one train service but beyond Europe international rail could brought back to the same problems that flying causes! This section is focused on international or intercity rail because the majority of commuter and metro rail systems don't offer any incentive to book tickets in advance, and, in the majority of cases, are not competing in any way.

First of all trains typically follow the same route as models planes however, with less extreme price of the day, and less expensive deals when booking in advance. In the case of a train ticket that runs from New York City to Washington DC in advance could cost you $40. Booking that same day of departure will cost $200 but with gradual increases within.

If you're not sure about what the difference is or why traditional and budget airlines being separated, it's simply due to the different approach regarding how to reserve them and the fact that certain people view "flying" to be only with their favorite airlines, while others think that any route is possible that could end with you taking the cheaper option.

Buses

Buses are a subject of ridicule especially within North America, but they're an incredible asset. When flying is expensive in the airport's facilities jet fuel and aircraft (Which could cost millions of dollars) and trains come with specific tracks with a hefty upkeep costs, buses are large vehicles that transport passengers from one place to another. The savings are often evident, but it doesn't mean that buses are inexpensive.

Megabus is owned by Stagecoach and every bus will be equipped with at least one seat for PS1.

This is due to the fact that in many instances, buses can be the most efficient or only option. In addition, certain buses are more comfort focused, which could be the most smooth option, with the largest legroom. In Japan for example, the buses are commonly referred to as limousines and provide you with the most comfortable way, but with a price higher than you would expect.

Buses are usually reserved in advance in order to get the most affordable rates, however unlike other ways, the cost for not making a reservation in advance is less expensive. It could cost you triple the cost if you book on the day prior to, compared to paying 5x or 10x for flights or trains. Remember this when you are absolutely required to adjust your plans.

Helicopters, boats

The most fascinating transport options are only available in certain areas however it shouldn't be stated that since buses are the best option for budget travel and planes are the most efficient, it's not worth a look at these options! Personally, I've yet to go on more than a couple of simple ferry rides and if the transport is an attraction in itself for you, there's no reason to be embarrassed investing in this one and be thankful that's the exact thing you're doing and that it's not in the budget.

It is always advisable to make reservations prior to time, as helicopters could cost as little as 1/5 of the price of the entire trip if booked in advance for a trip to Monaco for instance. Always remember that flexibility equals money.

The Resting Place

Therefore, it is imperative to state right away that hostels are your best and only choice when you are looking for a bargain at costs, and also want to enjoy to enjoy the benefits of staying in a place (so you can share the room) This will always be the recommendation given to youngsters, and with reasons. Because hostels are available in the same locations like hotels. This portion of the guide will show you the best ways to get them cheaply by think of it as an "low cost hotel" The first step is the basic guidance and then the cutting down on cost.

Hotels are a place that everyone has a preference for and that preference is formed by the years of negative experiences or the stories of negative experiences at the very least. When I began flying on random flights or "travelling" to different countries around 18 , with no the experience of a hotel I was able to try a variety of experiences to gain a sense for the world.

In the beginning, despite my previous comments, I've had there were some unpleasant hotel experiences. Hotels that were not clean or didn't have air conditioning during the summer are the worst. However, staying in a place where the water was a green color, with a distinct scent of the hotel was probably the one I'm hoping to never surpass. I'm mentioning this because it was a four-star hotel, located in Kiev If you're interested, click here.

In reality 5 star hotels are usually the most shabby.

This is because the star rating of an hotel is often the most important piece information about it, aside from possibly its location or internet accessibility. But the reality is that in a lot of countries (with certain exceptions) the city hotel is not governed by no standard way to rank hotels, and in reality the star ratings themselves are self-imposed. One of the most intriguing ways to establish this is that many hotels have various star ratings, based on the site you're looking it out on.

If a hotel is rated five stars, it could have put lots of energy to provide 5 star service and gorgeous lobby decor to make you feel as if it's five stars. But some of the most important amenities at a hotel, like in-room USB ports, speedy Wifi or easily controlled lighting requirements complete overhauls for an old hotel (which tends to be the case when they choose not to cover) however, the majority of budget hotels are much more modern and are not included because they are available when they first built and erected the hotel.

Therefore, the condition of a hotel's building could be a good indicator that older hotels are more likely to have wear that isn't fixedand can be an outdated definition about what "hotel" is.

Furthermore, the more luxurious the hotel is it, the more comfortable they are that they are able to sell you something when you're there, even if you pay higher for the rooms. You want access to wi-fi? 20 dollars a day. Breakfast? $30. It's also due to the loyalty programs these hotels offer that offer helpful "upgrades" to members who are elite that are offered at less stars hotels for free!

One of my favorite hotels for a single guest is EasyHotel even though it's not the most beautiful room you'll ever have the room is certainly not it's a consistent hotel with cozy beds, and always convenient areas. This is only one example however, so until you've developed your own taste of what you want from the hotel, you should definitely test around a bit - I'm still a fan of trying various chains and hotels as I can.

It is recommended to look up Google Maps rating. Google Maps rating, or in fact any other user-generated review site, can provide you with an unreliable number until you realize that there are two distinct star ratings , one for what the owner believes it's worth, and another that those who visit it consider it worth. Since I began doing this, I've yet to stay in an awful hotel!

Okay, so here's the way to stay in an excellent hotel. Set your minimum bar , and adhere to it. However, what do you do to find the best hotel for an affordable cost?

It is best to consider the loyalty you earn by staying with a particular chain. Some of the biggest chains have programs that offer cutbacks and benefits for staying for a set amount of nights. this could seem like an attractive reward, but this is only an option to consider if you have time short and the chain really meets your needs for a hotel and you're looking for consistency in each city.

If saving money is the thing you're after (as the title of this guide suggests) then what you can look into is an independent hotel aggregator, and searching using them. This lets you see each room that is available for the night you're looking for - and then to evaluate the costs as well as star ratings and distance from the centre to determine which one is best for your needs.

The majority of them are alike in price, but I personally prefer hotels.com for speed and convenience is what I want as I'm already familiar with their website . Every 10th night you stay there you get an 11th night for free (which I do several times per year) but because there are so many seasonal deals and new websites, it's worth a look through them all to find the best option for your first choice.

Whatever the case the best thing I would recommend, for those with a bit of time to spare is to use an aggregator of hotels. This may sound like a joke however since every site could have slight price and fee differences and charges, it's generally beneficial to find a website that chooses the most affordable possible option for every hotel and then plots them on maps.

This is the way I would recommend to ensure you get the best cost for hotels, but also to take distance into the calculation. The most straightforward option can be Google Hotels (as it works with Google Maps, that you probably already use) However, sky scanner could be worth a look as it will be used to combine flights and hotels in order to obtain a complete price for the trip.

Before I leave, I try to determine the location of the central point, or at least the middle of where I'm going to go, because one of the most common mistakes when sorting through price is finding a great accommodation which is located 45 minutes out from the centre. This is most often the case in larger cities.

As time is money and in certain circumstances taxi rides may be needed. This could be more costly than a hotel room, so I would suggest you read the section on how to get around if you're looking to master this. But, it's not difficult to simply stay close to public transport if are planning to utilize this, such as a central station or any other transport hubs marked "central."

It's generally worth paying an extra bit to be near these places, but the real value lies in seeking to be within 5-10 minutes of these places. You'll be able to see authentic local scenery along the way and save the cost of transportation which is typically much more than the amount you'd pay for a five minute walk to the city centre.

Therefore, the most effective way to save money , other than simply choosing the best value between location and price and comfort, is what's known as the "travel hacking" aspect. It's not all legally acceptable however, it's definitely worthwhile to know about at the minimum.

By signing up on each website and searching for hotels in the cities you'd like to stay in will typically result that can be discounts. I receive regular emails from the majority of them, with discounts of up to 5-20.

Certain hotels offer breakfast free of charge which can help make it easier to eat the food you have to pay for. This is a common practice however, the aspect you're not hearing of is the fact that hotel don't often have lists of who's going to breakfast , which means you can have a great breakfast for no cost.

The second aspect is that, if the hotel has a policy of checking the rooms in the hotel, you can go to a different hotel and, as long as seem like you belong to the hotel, you are able to eat breakfast in a variety of major hotels for no cost! * (Depending on your moral character there could be some guilt attributable.)

Find a room rooms for greater (or less) persons - always consider looking for rooms that are 1 person as opposed to rooms for two people depending on whether single or with a couple. The majority of rooms with two persons are less expensive or have similar to the price, however they offer more space and the option of a double bed.

Sometimes rooms with one person are less expensive due to the hotel taxes imposed by cities. Although everyone agrees that you must pay taxes, are they actually required to pay tax to an international government in addition to the entry fee to the country? This is the ethical issue that you must decide for yourself. It can be raised when AirBNB is considerably cheaper in the area, since it may be due to similar reasons.

Special notes. I've for a long time not made use of this option for booking online, however it turned out that it is possible to get a lot from it. You can ask for an upgrade or more spacious flooring (or lower) and declare it your anniversary and receive special services...

Consuming food

The main factor in deciding which restaurant to go to is based on the individual's preference. It's therefore difficult to give definitive recommendations and suggestions in this area - however, should you want to reduce your expenses while enjoying tasty and intriguing food, this is my approach to achieve that goal;

Avoid eating out - I'll admit that it's been awhile since I was a huge fan of the idea. Particularly when you're not with anyone else in a place, it's an option to pay extra money for adding five steps to your dining experience in a way that even places that aren't expensive charging huge sums after drinks and food are added to tipping and tax and service charges. The only thing you get in a restaurant is space , not the food. It's good sometimes but not always..

Although it's an enjoyable experience however, the majority of locals don't take advantage of these eateries regardless, and in a city that is a tourist destination, there's a lot of high-priced foods in places that may not be appropriate. For a great example of this, in UK, in the UK "fish as well as chips" is best served at a store specifically for PS4 or PS10; however, the typical London restaurant can offer these two items (in completely different ways) for the PS30-PS40 range.

"Fish and Chips" Fish and Chips

Fast food is a great option if you're looking to consume the least amount of time eating out an amazing experience is to sample regional fast-food. A majority of countries have a massive network (such as Russia with Kruska Kartoshka the chain that is primarily for baked potatoes that are microwaved) and this is one of the most local experiences that you can get.

A visit to the nearby McDonalds is something that I find fascinating, since the menus differ between countries. The menu in Spain you can purchase beer along when you eat as well. In India there is none of the beef products. However, there is no beef in Japan

McDonalds is considered to be more than a high-end food and is advertised and priced accordingly!

Street food is believed to be a trend in the modern age but if you're trying to discover a fantastic recipe look for a chef who is committed to the dish for excellent outcomes. My favorite example can be found in Singapore where Michelin recognized restaurants cost between $3 and $4 for their food, and the most delicious Chicken rice available on the island (according Google's rating system) cost $3SGD for one small bowl or $4SGD for a big bowl. That's right, it's the best food available priced lower than big mac prices.

In general the best suggestions include being aware of your local rate of conversion and then check the menus to find any "splurge" restaurant before you go, you can be more flexible with the food that is less expensive. I prefer to create a small budget every day for trying new food items, and that is also a good system.

How to get around in a City

If your destination is an urban area, a large town or simply a metropolitan area, you'll require a way to travel around it. The cost is something that a lot of people don't consider and getting 10 taxi rides every day is going to drain your pocket very quickly.

My first suggestion here is to look up the city you're headed to take a look at the cost of travel into whether the ticket is worth the price or not. An hour-long taxi ride towards the center of the city? Most likely not worth the trip. A great airport, and walking distance of the center? It might be worth $10 extra to travel there.

This is mostly down to research, but because there are a variety of methods in each city, let's discuss the mixture that keeps costs low while still being fun.

Public transportation is great in cities with an efficient network, since it's usually cheap and "the most efficient method" to travel in the event that you find difficult. It typically takes the least effort and lets you move around at your own pace generally.

One of the ways I typically determine if a network is good and a poor one will be that they use "smart" or disposable tickets. These tickets allow you to purchase cards that rechargeable to place value on and then you can spend the money using your card when you go to any tram, bus or metro entry point.

Japan's Suica card (and any other IC card issued in Japan) is not only able to be used to effortlessly transfer money to a transport company and other services, but also in convenience stores!

The process is simple and flexible, and there is an entanglement between a system such as this and a well-functioning public transport network that is underneath it.

So , I typically recommend using the tram and metro, regardless of budget since they'll usually be more efficient than taking taxis for 10x less. Buses also have an image of being a scourge for certain individuals. In reality, buses are the cheapest stop gap option within a public transportation system and a taxi is likely to be more efficient and flexible , but it will come at a much higher cost.

If your aim is to stay clear of that price (I doubt you would have reached this point in a tutorial on how to save money it weren't) Let's discuss taxis.

Taxis are costly. In almost all cases, with bizarre stories and even countries such as Cuba where taxi drivers earns more than an MD, there's a lot of profit to be made transporting people to places, most likely due to monopolies of taxi licenses. For example, New York City has only 13,000 licenses in an area of more than 8 million residents, which means that businesses are basically assured at all costs.

There are nations like Singapore where taxis are deregulated and can cost between $5 and $10 to traverse the entire country, in the majority of other countries you must choose between Uber or taxis Uber, which is the more convenient and less expensive alternative - while taxis tend to be more responsible.

In Bangkok The color of the taxi's exterior tells you what kind of deal you'll receive! This is the one you should be looking for.

No matter which method you decide to go, ensure you research thoroughly and are aware of the price you can expect and also how reliable the service will be. Taxi prices vary widely between countries however uber usually has a lower cost.

The decision for me is simple, however this is an excellent stop-gap measure for short to medium distances. even if you don't plan on driving through the entire region, it's more practical to use Uber (or some other service that allows ridesharing) rather than hire cars.

Chapter 10: How To Fly Free

Although the above may sound appealing, you might want to ask yourself 'Well, okay however, how can you pay for the plane ticket there? Yes, flights to distant destinations can be costly However, I'll show you an effective method to turn your trip into an inexpensive venture.

Here's how you can get started. Start by getting various card that are travel-related. As you make regular purchases, you'll earn points. You will then receive frequent flyer points. In the near future, the miles you've earned could cover an entire trip Asia, Europe, Africa and wherever else you'd like to travel to. If you're not able to accumulate enough miles for flyer tickets at no cost but at the very least, you'll receive them at a massive discount, making your trip an easy one. You use money every each day, therefore I highly recommend using the credit card for travel to make all purchases. All you need to remember is that you should not spend any more money than you can afford and also make sure you can pay your expenses. So long as you keep doing these things, you is your ticket to flying at no cost. If this wasn't enough info for you extrapackofpeanuts.com has a great article on frequent flyer miles.

Another plan is to purchase airline credit cards. If you mix them with a reward card you'll end up with a low-cost flight soon.

If the thought of enrolling for credit cards isn't appealing for you (although I would highly recommend that you sign up) there are many other options alternatives to make an affordable travel deal in no time. The most effective option is to sign up for a variety of airline newsletters. They typically offer special deals and discounts. Be alert for deals that offer 2-for-1. Here's an example: one of my friends was watching a demo video of United Airlines and surprisingly he was awarded free 1,000 miles for his next journey. Other companies, when you purchase items from them, will also offer miles for free (they must sign a collaboration contract with the airline they want to use). It is important to know the restaurants, companies and fashion boutiques. provide these bonus points/miles for free.

Another option is to purchase from large online stores such as Amazon, Target, Apple and many other websites that give you miles. For each cent you pay for items you purchase, you'll earn four miles. Imagine you make purchases of of $1,000 over a period of several months. You'll end up with the option of accumulating up to 4,000 miles. Additionally, you can pay for an entire journey between Chicago from Chicago to Los Angeles. As you can see, buying things with a credit card offers more advantages for you today. You don't need cash to purchase things by credit/debit card, and earn rewards mileage and points.

If you are in Europe certain airlines offer discounts and sales but only a few customers pay the full cost. There is always an affordable ticket just as much as the taxes! Take a look at Ryan Air, Easy Jet, Fly Monarch, Jet Star and Virgin Australia. Additionally, you can use Skyscanner or Momondo to search for low-cost hotels and flights.

Cheap flights are often booked during times when there is no season. It is the time when few people are planning to travel to anyplace, such as in the fall, when temperatures are not comfortable and people are returning from holidays and vacations. It is possible to find it difficult to travel during this time however, it is worth taking into consideration. In this respect, on a typical day, the price of the flight can be different with a the difference of several hundred dollars. This means that certain night flights could be significantly cheaper than daytime flights.

My most-used method of finding tickets at a bargain is to visit Kayak, Momondo and Skyscanner. I make sure to check all of these websites to determine which ones have the best rates. They collect data from all airlines and suggest the most suitable option for the flight you want. One thing that's essential when searching for low-cost tickets is to set your internet browser in Incognito Mode. Airlines typically have the exact flight that you've searched for previously and will increase the cost by a small amount. However, with Incognito mode, you'll be unidentified and they will change prices without being affected by your searches.

On the websites mentioned above, they generally have a flex button that allows you can view all prices for the entire week or month at the time you are planning to fly. This is an enormous benefit for you. I've had flights that cost $400 for flights on Fridays and 50$ on Wednesday. The price difference is huge.

What time do you need to make your booking? This is the most frequent question people have. In the past, I've been looking for a long time. This particular airline states that you should make reservations 8 weeks ahead of time, but regular travelers recommend booking 6 weeks ahead. It is not advisable to make a booking too far in advance or too early before your flight.

Where to Find a Place to Stay

This is a breeze. The answer is simple: Couchsurfing. It's a way to stay in a place that allow you to meet people and sleeping in a cozy and warm space. Contrary to AirBnB which is a rental service, you do not have to pay for a single penny to stay in someone's home. Many people are aware of this and are more than willing to let a exhausted traveler stay in their home for a number of nights. It is important to, of course be respectful of your host's confidence. Many great stories are born out of this. The hosts are often travelers themselves, which means you're assured that they've got some amazing stories to share.

Other websites that offer free couchsurfing include Hospitality Club, Be Welcome and Servas. In the moment, Couchsurfing has become the one most well-known.

Another option for lodging is to consider an exchange of houses. This basically means that you swap your apartment or house with someone from different country (your intended destination). A good place to start is websites such as Home Exchange, Home Exchange Vacation or Home Base Holidays. There's also the option of renting your house while on the road. This can be considered to earn money that will fully fund your journey.

A small but meaningful method to stay in a place (with the possibility of walking around) is to make use of Housesit. What this means is you can reach out to anyone planning a trip away from home and offer them to take care of their house. It's a win for you as that you don't have to pay and you'll are able to spend time walking around, exploring and generally get to explore your dream destination. It's a win-win situation for everyone involved and that's why it's gaining recognition. Websites offering these services include

House Carers, The Caretaker Gazette and Mind My House.

If you're searching for alternatives in Australia it is recommended to take a look at House Sit World, Happy House Sitters and Aussie House Sitters. Sometimes, posting an advertisement on sites like Craigslist or Facebook can assist you in finding the right match. Don't be afraid to look at other alternatives such as university communities and message boards, newspapers from universities and all kinds of community or local centers.

The monasteries and religious sites can be a great option for lodging. It is possible to request to stay at no cost, however, you must offer an amount of work. Be aware that they are generally basic and offer just beds and a desk. In some monasteries , you'll need to pay (prices differ widely from $50 to just a few dollars per night) So make sure you make sure you check before leaving. If you have the ability to speak with them directly it is best. If not, look for communities with specific details about the subject.

Extra tip: One thing worth pondering can be found in the next. Let's say that you reach your destination. You're in a hostel dormitory. This is how you can get the room. You can ask the manager of your hostel some tasks in the hostel for the cost of your room. You can choose to lower the cost of your room, or, if you're extremely lucky you may be able to stay free for the duration of your working time. If you've worked in the hospitality industry the chances of you being successful are significantly higher. Whatever option you choose, you must ensure that you have a valid work visa and permit prior to when you start working. If not, it's illegal.

How do you work from your home

This strategy works for lots of people, and it's extremely rewarding. It allows you to work and earn money (virtually while traveling and having enjoyable) Also, you are able to connect with the locals. You discover things about them that you would not be able to do if you were a normal tourist. Of course, the majority of jobs abroad might not appeal to those who are interested, but if put aside your pride for a few days you'll be perfectly.

Here are some possibilities to consider:

- Bartender

- Waiter/Waitress

- Hotel/Hostel worker

- Au pair

- Tour guide

- Casino employee

- Ship/Yacht Worker

- Farm worker

" English (other languages) teacher

There's plenty more options to this list, but this is a good starting point to help you get started. Certain of these jobs could be exclusive to certain regions (farm worker is very popular among New Zealand and Australia) While diving instructors requires certain certifications. For many , the teaching of English is a fantastic beginning. Many returned home with a wealth of money after just a few months teaching abroad. You still have time to wander around the area or even the city. It is not necessary to be working full-time as you earn enough to cover the essential expenses.

As I said, the ship or yacht worker I'm sure to explain a few additional details about it.

As a worker, you need to think "work any job" from Cook to navigator's assistant and so on. Whatever your individual skills are they can be utilized in the workplace. Websites like UK Crewseekers offer options for many different employees. Review these suggestions. Similar to this, and perhaps more adventurous , is to visit the port nearby and ask for help. It might seem like something out of the movie of a pirate however, it's worthwhile to try.

Also, never forget to consider (and know how to better understand) how the weather will affect your seasons. There's this concept of'repositioning crossings' which implies that based on specific conditions (good conditions and not an storm) the vessel is sailing. The owners of ships and boats take the changes into consideration and some times of the year are better than other. Also, take some time looking into this and then try to find that season's best time to start when it begins.

Consider cruise ships the same way. Although it might not be as thrilling as boats, but it's as profitable and effective.

Guidebooks for tours may be specific to specific locations, and you may require a familiarity with the area But what about a trip planner? It doesn't need anything particular or intricate. It's all you need to do is think about the whole trip: the location where your group will go to, what they'll be seeing, when each of these events occur in place, etc. It's that easy that even people with no prior experience can manage it. In the end, you can visit someplace in the world at no cost (or at the very least, for massive savings). It's the travel companies that finance these trips, and they have hired people to assist with the organizing. If my story has inspired you, you should check out for the

Adventures Incorporated and Adventures Abroad websites.

If you are looking to teach English (or other languages) here is the ideal spot. If you're proficient in English and are fluent in it, you will likely be able to get a an employment as a teacher within a matter of minutes. What is your mother tongue? You can also teach that! It might even be more compensated since it's one of the few languages that many people are aware of. If you're proficient in English however it's not your primary language, you might need certain certifications like the TEFL or Cambridge certificate (or similar). It's not necessary, however, if you're certain of your proficiency. Of course, evidence of this is always beneficial and most appreciated.

It is important to determine your strengths and then find a way to share it with other people. Perhaps you're a computer expert or are a designer, software engineer and so on. You can advertise yourself as an expert in these areas and showcase your knowledge. Remember that emerging countries (mostly those in Asia) are looking for instructors in a variety of fields.

In addition to work, you might think about the possibility of volunteering to help an organization. Consider opportunities for volunteering in the region where you plan to travel. Yes, volunteer work is hard work and requires perseverance, dedication and time, however you will receive accommodations and meals. Certain fundraising initiatives can assist you in obtaining cash to spend on yourself, so think about this as well. For a start, check the following websites: United Nations Volunteers, Voly and HelpX.

Charity, volunteer... These are all hot subjects among travelers however, there's a different one in the same vein, that might appeal to more avid readers. This is about setting yourself a goal and locating sponsors. It's all for a worthy cause, because it's charitable work however, you also get to undertake something extremely difficult, such as the climb of Mount Everest, diving in deep oceans and seas that aren't explored and so on. Whatever is on your mind and what you've always wanted to do and now you can have the chance to try it. Take a look at Global Adventure Challenges, Charity Treks and Across the Divide. It is important to note that if you've never been on a similar adventure before (e.g. climbing mountains at high altitude or extreme diving) sponsors might view it as too big of a risk to your health and will not offer the money. If you don't, you could spend some time preparing before applying with some previous experience.

Bonus suggestion: Have a look at WWOFing. This is basically a voluntary working on a farm of someone else's. You are asked to help out with the farm's work and in return, you're provided with food and lodging. It's based in the spirit of mutual respect and assistance. If, for instance, you plan to stay in an Italian rural village or region, the average cost for accommodation in a hostel is EUR18 daily. If you intend to stay for two months, you'll have to pay at least EUR2,000. If you make use of WWOFing, you will be able to reduce this amount and enjoy a an unforgettable experience.

The only fee you need to pay is the membership fee, which is around EUR25. Keep in mind that for different countries this cost could differ due to the local farmer's associations.

How can you afford to eat?

It's true that eating out wherever it is (home or overseas) isn't always easy. It's not something you could get for free and very rarely any person will provide you with food for free day in and day out. This may happen once the course of time, but it's certainly not over the long run. How do you deal with it without breaking your bank account off?

Perhaps you're already aware of the expensive cost of dining in countries with high standards. In some less expensive locations, there is no need to go to expensive restaurants and meals are inexpensive. However, what can cost you less is cooking your own meals. You will save over 50% of the cost when you cook your meals by yourself. If you are staying with the home of a couchsurfing host, or the Housesit arrangement there is a good chance that you'll have access to an kitchen. If you don't intend on (or do not like) staying in other people's accommodation, ensure you have cooking utensils and silverware, so that you can at least cook sandwiches to take with you.

Buffets are a great and affordable option to dine out. You can fill your meals with whatever they have on provide. Restaurants or eating places offer substantial discounts on food and drinks before they end their hours. There may be some meals that were not sold during the day, and to ensure to not throw it in the garbage the restaurant offers it affordable (more than 50percent discount). Keep in mind that this isn't leftovers, but the actual meals that were cooked on the next day.

How to save money while you spend your time

Okay, you're in a couch with a friend, but the next day, if you're looking to get out and explore the area what should you do?

If you've never had the pleasure of hearing about Free Walking Tours, you should now hear about it from me. This is a popular method in the majority of large European city and major cities and also in Asian cities, Australia, New Zealand, as well as within New York. Take the time to research the cities in which (along the route) you can avail the walking tours for free. In this respect one of the organizations that provide free walking tours include Australia Free Walking Tours, Athens, Bratislava, Brasov, Big Apple Greeters (in New York) and New Europe Walking Tours (for European travels). Simply type in Google ' Free walking tours'.

The rental of a campervan is another way of cutting off the cost of taking buses or trains. Although some trains provide cheap tickets, they will cost more than what you're willing to pay. If you lease the (mini)van you can sleep, travel as well as cook inside it. It is possible to do this for just thirty dollars per day.

If you're interested in the idea of hiring an automobile to travel then you can utilize Gumtree to find fellow travelers. It is possible to lower the cost per person when you travel with a friend. The cost is shared between fuel and the rental of the vehicle. For some travelers (or your own) you could use this as a way to get from one location to the next and then purchase gas.

The city tourism cards are beneficial when you are planning to take part in a variety of things in the city that you will be visiting. For instance London. It is much less expensive to purchase "The London Pass" that includes London Eye, London Zoo, Tower of London and more than 60 other attractions included in the ticket. The pass is much cheaper than buying each ticket separately. The cards can be bought in any travel agency or airports. You can also purchase them online. These include costs of all types and therefore can help you save hundreds of dollars. Some (in certain countries) could even provide free public transport.

The main purpose behind this card is to grant you access to the city's most well-known attractions. In addition, the cards might also offer discounts in shops and restaurants. Based on the location you're in and the city in which you're going the card will offer you a variety of discounts and offers. Some will offer more, others lesser, however the main point of the concept is that the visitor is able to enjoy more and spend less. Most of them activate upon first use and must be utilized within day (up for 72-hours).

Chapter 11: The Research

Once you've decided on your trip at a general basis (budget length, length, location and the style) It is now time to begin researching the details. It is recommended to begin your research with a reasonable amount of time advance. If you're planning an entire year of travel, begin looking for information about 5-9 months ahead.

Be aware that you're not making any bookings in this moment This is to conduct research.

If you're searching for flights on a site but you must be aware that there is a difference between the types of sites are created equally. Because you've got an idea of the type of vacation you're planning to go on at in the near future, you'll be able to identify the type of travel websites which will be the most useful for you.

While you research, think about the cities you would like to see in each area that you arrive in. The less tickets you purchase the better, so be sure to visit each city you'd like to visit ensure that you don't have to return to catch a different flight. Be sure to verify your frequent flying miles.

It can impact the airline you choose to fly with and can will save you lots of dollars. There are many websites that offer cheap flights, however they are among the most reliable:

Bing Travel

Yapta

Kayak

Hipmunk

Bing Travel is a good site due to its "price predictor" that is intended to give you advice on the likelihood that airfare will rise or fall.

Just type in the destination and the website will show up flights, along with suggestions on whether to hold off or purchase tickets now. Naturally Bing Travel's suggestions are not the word of God. It is important to note there is a limitation to Bing Travel only works in the United States, so if you reside outside the US and you are planning your next excursion, you should look elsewhere on the website.

Yapta is an excellent website if you're looking to receive a refund on a flight in the event that the price drops when you purchase the ticket. Yapta will notify you when the price of your flight drops and if the airline isn't able to refund you (if you pay less than an amount), Yapta will help you determine the best way to get your refund.

Kayak is a well-known site and has a great deal of information. With the Explore tool of Kayak allows you to view an international map that lists the best destinations for you within a set price per flight ticket. You can also pick the best timing for your flight, activities and even the weather. You will get the most value out of Kayak when you're flexible with your schedule and location.

Hipmunk is a relatively new website and is focused on plane trips. While many sites focus on price and view an hourly flight of $300 as superior to an hourly flight of $400 however Hipmunk functions more like a human. It categorizes flights according to "agony," which factors in the price of tickets length, length, and layovers.

This website will also send you notifications about sales as well as monitor a specific flight to determine if the price decreases prior to purchasing.

If you're planning to go on a real around the world trip, it is recommended to consider purchasing around-the-world airline tickets. They can be extremely economical, however they are also subject to more regulations. They, for instance, generally arrange your flights in the same geographic directions which means you'll constantly be traveling either north, east, west or south. You'll need to determine your travel route and the places you wish to visit based upon the tickets you purchased for your flight.

The tickets also have a time-frame that is pre-set for stopping, so in the event that you wish to stay for longer in a specific city, it wouldn't be an option on the RTW ticket, unless you are willing to pay for a fee.

If you're not determined about a particular path and would prefer a more definite timetable, RTW tickets are a excellent alternative. They are designed specifically for students who are taking the "gap" year and will allow for enough travel for around 12 months.

If you're in search of lodging, many websites for flights (like Hipmunk) also offer hotel prices, however If you'd prefer a different website or simply want to compare rates, there are many choices.

This is the perfect time to start thinking on what style you'd like to travel in Super nice hotels, cheap hostels or something in between. Below is a list that includes some of the best hotels booking websites:

Priceline.com

Hotels.com

TripAdvisor.com

Hostelz.com

Priceline.com allows you to set your price, so you can use your budget in a literal way on this website.

When you search for a hotel, you must select the minimum star class as well as the duration you'll stay, the part of the city you'd like to stay in, and the amount you're willing to pay. The problem is that you do not know which hotel you'll be staying at until after you've booked it, which means it's like a blind auction , where you could be in a shabby area of town.

If you're an adventurous person and flexible in the direction you go This is a fantastic website.

Hotels.com is among the largest lodging websites there. It's also a fantastic site to search for deals that are last-minute or seasonal. It also offers an Welcome Rewards program, where you can earn points by staying in any of the 85,000 hotels that are members and also win a night for free.

This is especially helpful to those who frequently travel. It's similar to frequent flyer miles for hotels. To save money on food costs when you're at various destinations, search for hotels that offer breakfast for free.

TripAdvisor.com is a review website which allows you to see what real customers are saying about their experiences at hundreds of thousands accommodation options, not just hotels. It lets you know the place's ranking in terms of family-friendliness, value as well as business-friendly, luxurious and so on. This is useful as it gives you more information about the kinds of amenities you will purchase.

If you're committed to spending the least amount possible on accommodation, Hostelz.com lets you get an insider's view of over 54,000 hostels spread across 94,000 cities. Many hostels are now hotels however, they are much less expensive, which means you will find some fantastic offers on this site as well as read reviews from fellow travellers.

This website is a great option to feel confident in case you're not familiar with sleeping in hostels and are cautious about moving away from the traditional hotel experience.

Make your decisions

When you're comfortable with the flight and the hotels you've selected then take them off the list. Make sure you have plenty of time prior to the date of your trip to prepare for any other details and ensure that you get the flight and accommodation you need at the lowest cost.

The advantage of booking early is financial. When booking make sure you are flexible. There may be a better rate that comes on the day you plan to book, so choose that deal. The hotel you choose could have the two-nights and one free night offer.

The possibility of something major could come out, for example, one of the destinations you were planning to visit suddenly becomes hazardous or is affected by significant weather events which could impact tourism.

The point is, from the moment you click the "book" click, you should be open to changing things to suit your needs.

This is the perfect moment to think about other forms of transportation you may require, such as hiring a car or getting to destinations with a boat. Prior to booking flights, it is worth looking into whether driving could be less expensive than flying.

The site costtodrive.com allows you to input the current location and city along with the year, make as well as the model and year of your vehicle and informs you of the price to drive. If you're renting a car to travel, you'll need to take into account the price at the start of your journey.

If you aren't sure the cost of your car in the first place, you can gain an idea of what it will be to drive as opposed to flying. This is a great website to keep in mind since even if you decide to fly it is likely that you will traveling around, and it's always good to know how much your expenses will be.

After you have reserved your flights and hotels determine your budget for the next day. What is the amount you are going to spend on food? Activities?

Take into account the exchange rate of every country you visit.

It may seem complicated, but it's crucial. You don't want to arrive in a different country, only to pay more than you planned and you'll need to adjust the next destination. Create an Excel spreadsheet that contains the various exchange rates that you have calculated the days before departure so that you only need to enter the numbers prior to your departure to a new destination and the new exchange rate.

If you're in this stage, you should over estimate the amount you believe you'll spend on a daily basis. It's better to have some cash remaining than to losing money.

When you travel

It's much simpler to adhere on a tight budget when paying for certain costs such as hotels and flights, however it's harder when you're actually on the road and exploring all the amazing things to take in and experience. It is possible to get carried away and blow half your day's expenses on one thing.

If you find something that is interesting you find interesting, take a second to take a moment to reflect. Are there alternatives which is less expensive? Perhaps this is an event or meal that comes only once and you believe it is worth the cost?

To make sure that you're getting the most value for your money Do some research about the top tourist destinations and restaurants. Food and activities are usually expensive, so you should check websites to read reviews. But, at the same time do not just look at the price.

There are many things that could be more expensive than what your budget can afford However, do not get too cheap to are unable to enjoy something that could never get to go back to.

To cut costs, be aware of the culture of food in the country you're in. Many countries in Europe offer mineral water, not tap water, and they will charge you. Be sure to ask before they hand you glasses.

This is crucial particularly for Americans who are used to free water everywhere they travel. There are certain meals that are less expensive than other times; for instance, most restaurants during lunch are significantly cheaper than dinner time. Take a look at eating a substantial lunch in the afternoon, and stay clear of sit-down restaurants during dinner time.

Another option is eating at the bar and not asking to sit down since the same drinks and food at the bar will be less than dining at tables. Beware of menus, and seek out fixed-price menus or menus that are served daily, which tend to be less expensive than other menu items. When choosing the right wine, you should always choose for a wine that is local.

If you're on the move and become hungry, stay clear of the establishments near the main tourist destinations. They are the perfect spot for hungry and uninformed tourists and are likely to charge more for sandwiches than the café that is only a few minutes away.

When it comes to walking, you should be prepared to spend a lot of walking. It's a great way to exercise that will also help you save money for taxis, taxi rental and fuel. The majority of towns (especially located in Western Europe) are small enough to allow you to take in a lot by walking. Bring your best walking shoes.

Before you set out at dawn, make a plan for your route to give you an idea of the intensity of a workout you'll be getting, and where the closest cafes are, to ensure you aren't trapped in the middle of lunch.

Another reason for spending too much that happens to travelers is when they purchase souvenirs. Locals create tables and booths on the streets or in markets , and will charge expensive prices to try to lure tourists into a trap. They simply take out their wallets when they hear a call.

To not spend $50 on sunglasses that could be worth less than $10, you'll have to master bartering. It can be difficult for many however, most countries beyond those in the United States will be expecting that you bargain and not be put off.

They can use tricks such as claiming that they need to leave to make you feel rushy, or saying that the poster you are looking for is unique even though you saw thirty of them offered for sale right across the street. They also teach you tricks and stand your stand.

Most importantly, they are looking to sell So if you get an offer that you don't prefer, you should not act as if you're about to leave and the person selling is more likely to accept an offer that is lower. There are a lot of books and websites that provide more information on how to barter effectively and, if you're planning to buy from markets during your travels, make a commitment to saving money , and avoid buying the first price that is offered.

Alternatives for the budget-conscious

So far, we've provided information on hotels, flights as well as food and other activities for budget-conscious travelers but what happens if you're dedicated to thrifty shopping?

If you're a novice to hotels and non-red-eye flights, and you're ready to put your budget-consciousness to an international holiday. With the advent of the Internet today, you are able to make plans for a trip that isn't conventional.

www.ingramcontent.com/pod-product-compliance
Lightning Source LLC
Chambersburg PA
CBHW050025130526
44590CB00042B/1917